FAITH FACTS HISTORY SCIENCE and How They Fit Together

Rheinallt Nantlais Williams

TYNDALE HOUSE PUBLISHERS, INC.
Wheaton, Illinois

Bible quotations, unless otherwise indicated, are from the Revised Standard Version.

Library of Congress Catalog Card Number 73-93969
ISBN 8423-0839-3 cloth; 8423-0840-7 paper

First published in Great Britain by Coverdale House Publishers Ltd., London, England, with the title *Faith Facing Facts.* American edition published by Tyndale House Publishers Inc., Wheaton, Illinois, by arrangement with and permission of Coverdale House Ltd.

First printing of American edition, February 1974

Printed in the United States of America

To the memory of my parents,
who finished the course, having kept the faith.

Contents

Preface

This book develops the theme of a public lecture I was privileged to deliver at the University College, Cardiff, under the auspices of the D. J. James Pantyfedwen Trust.

As it was the intention of the founder of the Trust "to further the cause of religion" (which, I think we may safely assume, in his case meant the Christian faith), I have attempted to show that the believer, far from being an escapist or a dealer in theological antiques, witnesses to the most real and relevant fact man was intended to know. However, just as doctors tell us that they themselves cannot heal anybody, but at best can only remove obstacles to the working of nature, so also no claim is made here to "prove" faith. I am attempting, rather, to remove some of the hindrances to it; and this will account for the polemical character of so much of the discussion in these pages.

I write in the conviction that the supreme Truth, which man is unable to reach, has itself reached man by assuming human nature, and this fact constitutes the foundation of the believer's knowledge of God and of the good news to which faith is the response.

The limits of the discussion attempted in this work are to a great extent determined by the intention of the lectureship: "to appeal to as wide a circle as possible of fairly well-educated and cultured people." Hence the wish expressed by the trustees — that "a too technical treatment should be avoided."

This I have sought to bear in mind; some of the publications, however, to which reference is made in the notes are of necessity technical in character. But as I am addressing the layman, and not writing a book for students of philosophy or theology, the discussion at times concerns pronouncements made against faith in newspaper articles and on television, which a large number of laymen will have read or heard. I have also retained in a measure the colloquial form of address, with the hope that this will not offend the purist overmuch.

It will be seen that many aspects of our theme have not been mentioned in these pages, nor have I always given reasons for many of my assumptions, because the reader who wishes to pursue the argument in detail will have ready access to the relevant contemporary publications. A few of these have been noted at the back of the book. Even so, I admit that, in the words of Calvin, I have had "more regard to what my plan admits than to what the extent of this topic requires."

As our main theme is the *Christian* faith, it is to this "religion" I refer whenever (except in quotations) I write "the Faith." Similarly, "the Resurrection," without further qualification, refers to the resurrection of Christ.

CHAPTER ONE

Vital Faith

The great medieval figure Dante tells us that when he had lost Beatrice, he looked for consolation but found faith. He says that he was like a man looking for silver and finding gold. A thousand years before Dante's day, a Galilean fisherman had already made a comparison between faith and gold. But he said that even "more precious than perishable gold is faith which has stood the test" (1 Peter 1:7, New English Bible). And were it possible to bring together all the witnesses to this faith in the course of the last twenty centuries, we would be confronted with a very imposing spectacle indeed. It is the faith which has stood the test that will occupy our attention in these pages.

THE CENTRAL PLACE OF FAITH

Faith, in the vital sense of the term, is a key word in the Christian message. And if the claims made for it are true, it isn't surprising that it should be rated above gold, for it can bring man what gold is not able to buy. It was proclaimed as God's good news to the world, because it contained the secret of peace, freedom, and true fulfillment. St. Paul was commissioned to make it known to all nations, for without it man is an irredeemable failure. It is a fact of history that wherever its message was received, new life was born, a life filled with meaning and hope. It gave depth to life, and it fired those who possessed it to share with their fellow-men, far and near, what they themselves had received.

When we say these things about the Faith, we aren't simply romancing, although the history of the way the Christian faith has changed both human lives and human conditions from the time of its first appearance is unrivaled in the history of romance. But if this is the case, why should what brought healing to a sick world powerless to renew itself be so commonly regarded nowadays as the abracadabra of the clergy, a "childhood neurosis," the escape-hatch of those who find living in a world of hard facts somewhat heavy going? It can't be that man has hit upon some other solution for his troubles through progress in culture or technology or medicine. It seems obvious that the advances made in these directions have very little relevance to man's major ills. The ability to change the material conditions in which a man lives doesn't seem to have a parallel in his ability to change the vaster and deeper world within him. So, bedeviled by himself, man's most serious problem remains.

THE SKEPTICISM OF OUR TIME

Why, then, do so many shy away from faith? In reply to this question, we may mention three relevant factors. First is a widespread notion that facts discovered by "man come of age," as he is called, have exposed once and for all the futility of faith. "Facts are stubborn things," and a faith that cannot face them has very little chance of survival in the long run. Second, the word *faith* has by now been considerably devalued on account of its use in a diluted form, which lacks the power of the authentic thing found in the New Testament. The imitations of it which now abound cannot stand the test. Third, advances in the material standard of living, together with deterioration of those standards which have to do with man as a spiritual being, have resulted in blindness to the true meaning of life and, consequently, in failure to appreciate the need of the good news which the Christian message contains for man in every age.

We said that daylight scatters ghosts. The skeptic takes it

for granted that faith is one of those ghosts which has to disappear in the presence of facts. Yet we can't afford to ignore the fact that it was the Christian faith that brought to the world the very light which laid low so many of the ghosts that have haunted the lives of men throughout the ages. Moreover, that faith was itself born of fact: the fact of Jesus Christ. And faith, in the vital sense, was a response to him: the response of trust and commitment. The whole basis of faith was the person of Christ himself, not the ethical principles which he put into practice nor the high ideals he preached. It was the preaching of Christ, not of Christianity as an ethical or philosophical system, that gave power to the witness of the early believers. It was his person that inspired them from the beginning and made their message a gospel.

Of course, the name of Christ wasn't simply a sound without content. It did indeed contain "Christianity," but it also infinitely transcended it. He himself was the indispensable and eternal foundation of faith and of the life it inspired. He wasn't just a temporary scaffolding which would become irrelevant once the building was on its feet. The early Christian witnesses could never have dreamed of exhorting men to lead Christian lives by showing good will toward one another without first calling them to faith in Christ. It wouldn't make sense, for love, far from supplanting faith, is the living fruit of it. The first believers who took the Faith to the world were realists of the first order, realizing that a world which had failed the test of the ten commandments given on Mount Sinai hadn't the slightest hope of keeping the commandments given by Christ to his disciples on another mountain. The message of good news was proclaimed by men who had first known its power, and not simply been attracted by its principles. Were it not so, they would have cut sorry figures. They would be like a doctor who went around trying to heal others of a disease that he himself carried.

The implications of vital faith, understood as trust in Christ and commitment to him, will be seen more clearly when contrasted with other interpretations of the word *faith* which are still in popular use. Although some of these no doubt contain certain elements also present in what is specifically Christian faith, they lack what is central in the latter and therefore they are devoid of its vitality and power.

VARIOUS CONCEPTIONS OF FAITH

First, then, is the idea of faith as simply *firm conviction.* And on the face of it one might suppose that Christ himself endorsed this definition of faith. Didn't he say, "Whoever says to this mountain, 'Be taken up and cast into the sea,' and does not doubt in his heart, but believes that what he says will come to pass, it will be done for him"? (Mark 11:23). Few have been tempted to test these words literally, like the woman who decided to use such "faith" as a lever to remove a mountain which annoyed her by keeping the light from her bedroom. She muttered, "I thought as much," when it showed no sign of shifting! But many will "try it out" to remove other obstacles. Because it doesn't work with them, they conclude that its alleged power is pure fabrication. Here, for instance, is someone applying for a job he is eager to get. He decides to pull out all the stops, including what he regards as the prayer of faith — but to no avail. Has faith failed? Another test is the case of a sick man for whom fervent prayers of faith are offered with the firm conviction that they will be answered. But he dies. What becomes of the promise, "Whatever you ask in prayer, believe that you receive it and you will"? Has faith been discredited by facts? Or is it that not enough faith was exercised? Some will even say that it was simply a case of God answering "No." But the skeptic will conclude that it was just a matter of faith failing the test.

When we consider the words of Christ about faith in *their context,* we aren't left in doubt that much of what passes for faith isn't Christian faith at all. For Christ speaks not simply of the quantity of faith, but also of its quality. Hence, "If you ask for anything *in my name,* I will do it" (John 14:14). This means that faith in the Christian sense is not a device for getting what one wants. The logical impossibility of that is clear from the fact that if two persons with equal faith had set their heart on the same thing, at least one of them would have to conclude that faith didn't work. But "in my name" defines the nature of real faith. It means with Christ's authority, and consequently in accordance with his character, in his Spirit. It doesn't mean attaching the name of Christ to the end of our prayers. And to ask in his name implies that faith is no facile technique for the guaranteed success of self-interest. For the name of Christ isn't a magical word, an "open-sesame" that works whenever it is uttered with firm conviction. That the quality of one's spirit is relevant to the efficacy of prayer is brought out in the passage referring to faith that removes mountains. For Christ goes on to say, "And whenever you stand praying, forgive, if you have anything against any one; so that your Father also who is in heaven may forgive you your trespasses" (Mark 11:25). Hence, even the prayer for forgiveness, when offered in an unforgiving spirit, is a petition not in his name.

The true meaning of faith is further revealed by the fact that the faith which Christ rewarded with his healing touch was evidently meant to lead eventually to deeper trust that would result in the healing of the whole person, not simply of his body. The case of the healing of the ten lepers illustrates this. Christ himself commented on the sad condition of the nine, whose physical health had been restored, but whose self-centeredness had not been touched. Only one was moved to gratitude, and he alone had really been made well (Luke 17: 19). On another occasion, a superficial faith was met with warning rather than welcome: "You seek me," says Christ, "because you ate your fill of the loaves. Do not labor for the food which perishes, but for the food which endures to eternal life, which the Son of man will give to you" (John 6:26, 27).

Faith is also defined at times as a *receptive attitude* to truth: an ever-open mind that doesn't give up the search. One writer defines it as "a quest, an authentic search."[1] Now the Christian should always be open to truth, seeing that he believes that all truth coheres in Christ. But, as Gresham Machen puts it, the open mind is not "a mind with a hole in it," which can retain nothing. Moreover, *Christian* faith, far from being a quest for truth, is the direct consequence of what has already been revealed about the truth. That is why it entails both trust and commitment. To say that it is better to travel than to arrive is all right for one to whom life is just a jaunt with no particular destination. To change the metaphor, such a man would be like a person who, after being informed that there were no fish in the stream where he was angling, carried on regardless, on the grounds that it was the thrill of trying, not the achievement of catching, that he was really after.

To say that the Christian faith is a response to what has already come is not to say that the believer is therefore a big know-it-all. The man of genuine faith should be the first to recognize that he has much more to learn even of what he already knows, seeing that the mystery he "knows" surpasses knowledge. Nor is the Christian life a static affair in which the thrill of new horizons is absent. St. Paul tells us that the riches of Christ are "unsearchable" and only after he had seen the goal was he able to start the race of faith.

Faith is frequently regarded as a *submissive attitude* to a religious tradition, irrespective of any insight into the truth of what is believed. But it's clear that someone may be among the "faithful" in that sense without having faith in the Christian sense. Submission to tradition is not the same as submission to truth. There is nothing secondhand about New Testament faith, so it isn't surprising that the doughty champions of tradition were hostile to it. For faith is born of illumination and searching of heart. Its advent is a moment of truth. Vital faith is never mass-produced. Christ calls men by name, individually, to faith (John 10:3).

Another familiar conception of faith is that it constitutes *belief in a number of specific facts* made known by revelation. We don't for a moment dispute that real faith believes certain facts. It seems a far cry from New Testament faith to imagine that "you don't need to know anything about God in order to believe in him."[2] The Scriptures sanction no spiritual schizophrenia, in which piety and theology are allowed to go their own ways. Even so, nodding one's head even to Christian truth doesn't guarantee Christian faith. Nothing is specifically Christian about assenting to truth, for "the devils also believe, and tremble" (James 2:19, King James Version). In fact, the theology of the devils in respect to the person of Christ, for example, was more orthodox than that of the religious leaders

in Palestine. The devils believed, however, only *that* Jesus was the Son of God. They didn't believe *in* him. Their faith, therefore, was notional, not vital.

Sometimes faith is thought of as a *form of hope,* a temporary substitute for knowledge. Such faith is like a sailor clinging to his battered little craft which is being threatened by an angry sea, trusting he will eventually reach *terra firma.* Such hoping for the best, with the perpetual suspense it entails, knows little of the serenity and strength that characterized Christian faith when it was first proclaimed to the world. As Professor Hick rightly observes, faith is not just "a prudent gamble" but is in some sense a form of knowledge. St. Paul tells us that faith will remain when "knowledge" has passed away.

In some circles today, faith is defined as *"believing without evidence."* This cannot, however, be the meaning faith has in the New Testament. Believing without evidence would be a leap into darkness, a reliance on pot-luck. And since one patch of darkness is no different from any other, such a faith would be devoid of moral and spiritual significance. But in the Scriptures the call to faith is made on account of the light we have on the character of God and the condition of man. Faith has to do with "truth in the inward parts." That is why unbelief is regarded as a refusal to face the light, which exposes the real self for what it is (John 3:19). Hard though this saying is, it contains the clue to the whole point of the Christian message: it implies that the terms *faith* and *unbelief* do not, in the New Testament, represent mere intellectual viewpoints which believer and skeptic alike can hold without stirring from their seats in the grandstand. Rather, faith is essentially a response to the challenge of a revolutionary fact, and failure to see this is also failure to grasp the uniqueness of the Christian message in its profound and far-reaching character.

THE VITAL MEANING AND RELEVANCE OF FAITH

In the New Testament, faith has a number of meanings. Sometimes it means the *act of believing* something. It also means *what is believed,* as when we say, for instance, "the Christian faith." And occasionally it means *faithfulness.* But

these meanings derive their importance from the way they connect with what we have called vital faith: the faith which is, first of all, *trust and commitment.* The early believers weren't excited by the psychology of faith, whatever the fascinating ramifications of that study. Their concern was with the truth of the fact that awakened faith and with the vital response it elicited. That fact was an event. The event was the coming to the world of God's saving truth for man in the form of a personal, historical, concrete, and specific fact. This, declares the Faith, is the meaning of the event of Jesus Christ.

This event was proclaimed as a gospel because it was the means by which God would save those who believed. To many, however, the suggestion that the world needs a savior is scandalous. Isn't man his own savior? Isn't he winning the battle against the hostile forces around him — poverty, hunger, disease, ignorance? Aren't we living in days when humanism has good reason to rejoice in *its* faith: a faith that believes in the dignity of man in his own right, man with an "unconquerable soul," for which he need not "thank whatever gods may be"?

But the Faith presents us with a different picture of the human situation. The reason for this is not that the believer wishes to escape responsibility for cleaning up the world around him or for bettering himself and his fellow-men. The reason is that he is compelled to face facts that the humanist has omitted from his testimonial. These are the grim facts not about what is outside man, but with what things are like inside him. "Civilization," Dr. Moffatt, the missionary, wrote, "kills the tiger and breeds the fox." We see today that it can't do much about either. The tiger may take an occasional nap, but when he wakes up, he is the same tiger.

The scandal implied in the gospel isn't the creation of man's self-pity. It is forced upon him by brute fact. Why is it that when man gets more, he doesn't want to give more? How is it that increase in goods doesn't mean decrease in greed? What accounts for the strange fact that what man saves from want, he slaughters in war? The gospel makes no bones at all about the answer. It tells us that we are in breach of faith with the truth. Rot is deep down inside us. Cleaning the cup

outside, when fatal germs are left within, makes man a laughing-stock of devils. One New Testament writer puts the challenge bluntly: "What causes wars, and what causes fightings among you? Is it not your passions that are at war in your members? You desire and do not have; so you kill. And you covet and cannot obtain; so you fight and wage war" (James 4:1, 2).

But the Faith goes further than pointing out the corruption in the way we act. It doesn't beat around the bush in telling us that our *condition* is corrupt. We are, in St. Paul's words, "sold under sin" (Romans 7:14). To cast aspersions on our integrity is humiliating enough, but to question our dignity is unforgivable. But the gospel regards salvation as more important than soft soap. God will take care of our dignity. It is from him that it was derived. What we are obliged to do is to face facts. And the plain fact, says the Faith, is that man is a slave of guilt. To refuse to face this is to build one's life on a lie.

We can appreciate, therefore, why the believer isn't surprised to find Freud confessing: "I bow to the reproach that I have no consolation to offer." After all, the psychologist and psychiatrist have only human nature to draw upon. The object of faith, the God who inspires it, is not accessible to their techniques. But Faith itself speaks like this: "The life I now live . . . I live by faith in the Son of God" (Galatians 2:20). Those words weren't the words of a dreamer, but of one who was in touch with the source of things and whose whole Christian life was forged on the anvil of experience. He knew first-hand a stamina that could take "imprisonments, with countless beatings . . . toil and hardship . . . hunger and thirst . . . cold and exposure" (2 Corinthians 11:23-27) without cynicism or self-pity. Surely history has no record of a more inept designation than when St. Paul, the Apostle to the Gentiles, was referred to as "the apostle to the genteel"! Faith doesn't seek the consolation of a spiritual slumberland; its "consolation" is the revolution it brings. Only as the scandal of its message is faced may the good news it contains be realized. Just as the public ministry of Christ opened with the call, "Repent, and believe in the gospel" (Mark 1:15), so the last commission he gave was that "repentance and forgiveness of sins should be preached in his name to all nations" (Luke 24:47).

We have defined vital faith as a response of trust and commitment. Faith is response, because it is God's message, not man's cogitations, that awakens it. It is trust, because it is faith in a person who embodies the message, not in an abstract principle. It is commitment, because the response is the giving of oneself, not a case of lending a hand to a good cause.

In taking all, faith also undertakes to give all, which entails changing the center of gravity in the believer's life. This, however, is not a claim to sanctity, in the colloquial sense of the word. But it does imply a start in a new direction and some acquaintance with the "expulsive power of a new affection."

THE SOURCE OF FAITH'S POWER

It is undeniable that the sheer power both of the spirit of the early believers and of their actions was one of the most cogent factors in their witness for the Faith. Such power pointed to the fact to which their faith was a response. Without that fact, their faith would soon be going around with hands hanging down and with pretty feeble knees. There are, indeed, counterfeit faiths which attract because of the emotions they engender and the escape they temporarily provide from the acidity of life. "There is such a thing," Rickaby writes, "as a delicious oblivion of external realities and a joy in the workings of one's own mind; yet a dangerous joy, as is the joy of the inebriate, who in his transport is robbed of his property."[3] In contrast with such a condition, we find that the power which first "turned the world upside down" (Acts 17:6) through the preaching of the gospel was not something the early believers possessed themselves. Rather, their power came from the Spirit by whom they were possessed.

To illustrate this, we recall how, after performing a miraculous work of healing, the Apostle Peter answers the amazement of the crowd: "Why do you stare at us, as though by our own power or piety we had made him walk? . . . The Author of life . . . has given the man this perfect health in the presence of you all" (Acts 3:12, 15, 16). This, then, was the good news: that into a world where the writ of death had run throughout the ages, universally and inexorably, had now come the "Author of life." It wasn't good news *about* man, as the humanist offers, but good news *for* man. And this news came in the form of a man: one who fully embodied the truth of God, one who radiated its glory and imparted to those who believed something of its divine power.

So the event that first created faith was one no man could have planned or foreseen. The Christ had arrived unbidden on the human scene and from another direction. Although he pitched his tent among us, taking our infirmities and bearing our diseases, he addressed us from the opposite direction to that in which we ourselves were traveling. Hence, if nature were to produce a human being possessing the intellect of Plato, Aristotle, Kant, Einstein, and Russell all rolled into one, the gospel would still have to come to him as a word behind him saying: "This is the way" (Isaiah 30:21). For the Christian faith inevitably entails "turning around" for the man who believes.

Since faith is a power, a response, and not simply an intellectual stance, to ask whether it can stand the tests of reality is in fact to ask whether Christ is. Coming to faith isn't adopting a formula of self-inducement for "getting better and better every day." It wasn't "faith in faith" those early witnesses possessed, but faith in Christ. Hence, "everything is possible to him who believes" doesn't mean that everything is possible to him who believes that everything is possible, but rather to him who believes God's revelation in Christ. And so the apostle doesn't say, "I can do all things through believing I can," but "I can do all things in him who strengthens me" (Philippians 4:13). It is Christ who inspires the life of faith from start to finish (Hebrews 12:2, NEB).

EVIDENCE FOR THE TRUTH OF FAITH

We have sought to interpret the meaning of vital faith as set forth in the New Testament. But on what grounds did the first Christians claim that the truth of God had come in Jesus Christ?

We can only turn again to the records that are the source of our information in this matter. And there, in the New Testament, we read that the authority of Jesus of Nazareth was not a speculative fancy, but a living power communicated through the threefold medium of words, deeds, and presence.

The words of Jesus evoked the remark that "no man ever spoke like this man!" (John 7:46). And this isn't hard to believe. John tells us that Christ declared: "I am the bread of life; he who comes to me shall not hunger, and he who believes in me shall never thirst" (John 6:35); "I am the light of the world; he who follows me will not walk in darkness, but will have the light of life" (John 8:12); "Before Abraham was, I am" (John 8:58). In another Gospel we read about Christ's saying: "All authority in heaven and on earth has been given to me . . . and lo, I am with you always . . ." (Matthew 28: 18, 20); "Come to me, all who labor and are heavy-laden, and I will give you rest" (Matthew 11:28). Further, he claimed that he came to fulfill the law and the prophets, and that his truth alone could provide a foundation for life that would stand when all else collapsed. And above all, he claimed to be the truth which makes men free. Since he would give his life to ransom sinners, he had "authority on earth to forgive sins" (Mark 10:45; 2:10).

Astounding though such claims were, the response of those who heard Christ's words and believed in him was of such a nature that the Pharisees complained, "Look, the world has gone after him" (John 12:19). Peter declared that he had "the words of eternal life," and the "crowds were astonished . . . for he taught them as one who had authority" (Matthew 7: 28, 29). It was the authority of light shining in darkness. Christ needed no other light to illumine him, any more than one needs to strike a match in order to see the sun. Many, it is true, didn't recognize that light. The soul, like the body, can be afflicted with blindness. Nor is it difficult to understand why many fled from his light. It exposed the hypocrisy that boosts one's own ego by condemning the failings of others. It unmasked the pride that is puffed up with superficial piety. One thing is evident: there is nothing facile about vital faith.

Yet Jesus was no iconoclast intoxicated with his reputation

for shocking others and delighting in tirades against the religious humbug of his day. Huns can smash images, and you don't need an architect to drive a bulldozer. We read that he wept for those who rejected his message, because of the misery and fatal consequences of unbelief (Luke 19:41). The words he spoke in that context were the words of someone who cared, not of a spirit that condemned. So people marveled at "the gracious words which proceeded out of his mouth" (Luke 4:22). They were words that brought hope and healing to the rejected and dejected: words of "spirit and life."

Much praise has been lavished on the genius of Jesus as a teacher. His parables have been applauded for the skill of their artistry and the attractiveness of their simplicity. Yet it was their content, not their form, that really created faith. They tell of the father who sacrificed everything to bring the family home, despite the way they had behaved. His words penetrated deeper than the intellect, deeper than the emotions, deeper even than conscience. They unveiled hidden depths, where a man becomes aware of the purpose of his life, of the fact that he is lost, and of his need of a redeemer. They rang true to a woman who had failed to find fulfillment in her escapades with five husbands and the man with whom she was living when she met Christ. For that stranger at the well was the only one who had ever known her real thirst. His words rang true to Zacchaeus, who had risen in the world by stepping on the necks of his fellow-men, and who had become rich through extortion. The words of Christ to him accomplished more than any moralistic declamations or philosophic speculations. They brought salvation into his heart and the checkbook out of his pocket.

It will be seen, then, why we said that the consequences of authentic faith are profound and far-reaching. They are profound, because they transform the springs of action within. They are far-reaching, because the new spirit in the believer is to flow through him into every sphere of human relationships — social, political, cultural, religious. Nothing lies outside the jurisdiction of the real faith that has to do with man's relation to God and to his neighbor. Hence, Christ is the light of the *world,* not of the West, or of those who are religiously inclined.

The deeds of Jesus like his words, bore unmistakable witness to his authority. Alcott supposedly said to Carlyle that *he* could have said, "I and my Father are one," to which Carlyle replied that Christ got the world to believe him. One reason for this, apart from the fact that no man ever spoke like him, was that no man ever did the works he performed either. "We never saw anything like this!" (Mark 2:12) was the reaction of those who witnessed his great works. "He has done all things well," they declared (Mark 7:37). Jesus himself made it clear that his deeds were meant to be more than blessings to the individuals concerned. They were intended to be aids to faith throughout the ages. He said of the works he did in his Father's name: "They bear witness of me" (John 10:25). And on another occasion, in exhorting belief in his words, he added, "or else believe me for the sake of the works themselves" (John 14:11).

We read in the records that the works of Jesus showed how physical, human, and demonic nature recognized their Master in him. Even his enemies were compelled to admit that some superhuman power was at work in him. But their explanation was that he was a tool in the hands of "Be-elzebul, the prince of demons." On the other hand, a leading member of their council said, "Rabbi, we know that you are a teacher come from God; for no one can do these signs that you do, unless God is with him" (John 3:2). That the Be-elzebul theory was false is evident from the fact that the deeds of Jesus destroyed evil rather than encouraged it. His works were inspired by mercy, without a suggestion of any selfish motive. Need alone could call forth grace; not even moral merit could earn it. Class distinction had no part in his actions, for he would touch the untouchable and would stop in response to the cry of a blind beggar. On the one hand, a penniless woman (who for twelve years had been the victim of hemorrhage) proved his healing power, while on the other hand, the anguish of a nobleman (whose son was dying) was met by an act of mercy.

It was the authority of the *presence of Jesus,* that is, his person, that provided the final ground for faith in him. His words and works were only partial expressions of the mystery of his person. Confronted by him, many sensed the presence, not of a man of unusual genius and integrity, but of someone in whom the eternal God was manifesting his glory to mankind. Christ wasn't respected for his dedicated search for light; rather, he was himself the light. He wasn't admired as a champion of freedom; rather, he himself embodied freedom. No gap divided what he taught from what he was. And in that he stood alone. In him the world witnessed for the first time the "glory as of the only Son from the Father," the glory which was "full of grace and truth" (John 1:14).

But it wasn't until an event without parallel in the history of the world had been witnessed by the early disciples that the real mystery of the person of Christ was disclosed. Only then was the full significance of his coming to the world understood. That event was the resurrection from the dead of the crucified Jesus. The fact of the Resurrection is central in the Christian faith.[4] "If Christ was not raised, then our gospel is null and void, and so is your faith" (1 Corinthians 15:14, NEB).

To many today, such logic is unintelligible. How does what happened to the body of Christ affect the truth of his teaching? Surely, it is said, his noble example of self-denial and his exhortation to turn the other cheek cannot possibly die just because *he* is dead. To such an objection, the same witness gives a reply. In effect he says that a live example is of no use to dead men. And if it is a fact that we are dead in trespasses and sins, then the teachings of Christ cannot touch us. We first need to be made alive — alive to God. The sacrifice of Christ has to do with this need.

The main purpose of the Resurrection was to reveal the Jesus who suffered, as the Son of God who atones. It sealed the completion of his work. It indicated that his offering himself on our behalf was in fact God's way of redeeming us to himself.

On our behalf. This is indispensable for faith in the Christian sense, because we ourselves are neither able to come to God nor have we the right to do so. The Sermon on the Mount, without the sacrifice on our behalf on Calvary, would not have brought us to God or God to us. It would have been like giving a book on the art of swimming to a man who had already disappeared under the water.

We shall look more closely later on at the centrality of the resurrection of Christ as an event in history. Suffice it to say here that the first believers were commissioned to call the world to faith because of two central facts. The first is that the one to whom our faith is a response has opened for us a way to God through his victory over sin and death. The second is that he is alive for ever more, "never to die again" (Romans 6:9, NEB), and is now an abiding presence with those who have come to faith.

So in Christ the ultimate has become the most intimate. "The way, the truth, and the life," sought after by sages and argued about by philosophers, is here, and here to stay. Christ was proclaimed to the world not only as one who is alive and an object of hope in the future. Rather, he is the object of living trust here and now, since he has returned from the silent "beyond" and broken through the great divide of death. Hence, the message was a thing of power. The believers realized, not simply remembered, Christ as they met together for the breaking of bread and prayer (Acts 2:42). That their faith in him was no sentimental fancy was evidenced by the realism of their lives, the concern they showed for others, and the power of their witness.

The message of the Faith was to be for all men in every age. Fashions of thought change from generation to generation, but man remains the same. "Go forth to make all nations my disciples" (Matthew 28:19, NEB). That is good news for modern man.

CHAPTER TWO

Dynamic Fact

At one time it was taken for granted that believers and skeptics knew what they were disagreeing about when discussing Christian faith. But today we face two formidable opponents when we attempt to pass from the meaning of faith to its truth. One opponent tells us that the faith we have sought to define doesn't make sense. The other says it's out of date.

The charge that *faith in God does not make sense* is a weapon forged a few decades ago by a group known as logical positivists. Since that weapon is itself now somewhat out of date it may seem unnecessary to revive discussion about it. But modified versions of it are still around, and are very much in use. Although technically these versions have a different source, their purpose is so much like that of the original that they give the impression of becoming subsidiary products. They seek to expose the bogus character of the word *faith,* for faith is only possible on the assumption that God exists. But what has now been discovered, apparently, is that "God" is not so much nonexistent as devoid of *meaning*. Hence, a high-ranking officer in this theater of war has assured us that the labors of those who try to describe a reality which we cannot experience with any of the five senses "have all been devoted to the production of nonsense."[1] So the statement, "There is a transcendent God" does not, we are told, express a proposition at all.

What have atheists and the faithful been fighting about all

along, if even the key words in the debate have no meaning? How did they manage it? I suppose one can say that the reason for the fighting was that the contestants didn't realize they were only using blank cartridges. So although they were engaged in mock battles and no one was ever killed, emotions were being stirred because of ignorance of the facts.

A "LOGICAL" ATTACK: FAITH HAS NO MEANING

The charge that believers are using a word void of meaning when they talk about God is based on the apparent futility of applying any tests that would establish whether there was such a Being or not. In the case of all other supposed facts, there are ways of testing what we mean by affirming their existence. But believers persist in saying that *God* is a fact, whatever the findings of any possible tests may be. Suppose that two persons are in a room where the curtains haven't been drawn back, and one says to the other that outside the sun is shining. Yet when the curtains are opened, it's still dark in the room. Shouldn't the statement about the sun shining be retracted because facts disproved it? And if the one who made it were to say that he didn't mean the words in the sense the other meant, but nevertheless couldn't explain in what way he did mean them, wouldn't it be understandable if he was regarded either as a bit odd or as playing some game?

Now, take the statement that God is love. God, of course, cannot be seen with the eyes with which other objects are seen. The five senses are of no use to verify that statement in a direct fashion. But it will be said we know he is love because of the way he acts toward us. The skeptic will reply that love usually expresses itself in concern for the welfare of the loved one, yet the most cruel things are allowed to happen to those whom the heavenly Father is supposed to love. And this despite the fact that he is both omnipotent and all-good. To persist in holding on to the belief that God is love, when every test fails to show what it can mean, suggests to the skeptic that it doesn't in fact *mean* anything, but that it only expresses an emotion.

Obviously, if "God" is a meaningless word, to examine

evidence for his existence would be senseless. If I were to say that a bright red sound was sitting on my desk, no one in his right mind would set about investigating the evidence. If anything called for investigation, it would be my head, not my statement. The very logic of my statement would expose its nonsensical character: to look for evidence of its *truth* would be like looking for a square circle. Hence, it is said that "the meaningfulness of any transcendent realm . . . is the most critical issue for modern theology."[2]

AN ATTEMPT TO RESCUE FAITH

If God isn't a fact, faith must be a fiction that cannot expect to survive for long. And although some writers today have derived considerable comfort, it would appear, from salvaging bits and pieces that remain after the "wrecking of faith," their books would be of no interest to those who first taught the Christian faith to the world.

I have in mind those who wish to read a meaning into the Christian faith even when they have conceded that its talk about a God who transcends mankind can no longer be sustained. They say, for example, as Professor Braithwaite does, that what the Christian faith is *really* after is the recommendation of a certain way of living[3] — not of thinking about a being who is invisible, eternal, and completely beyond the world — and that the principle which should govern the Christian way of living is that of love. To many this now makes sense. It brings you down to earth and sets your feet on solid ground at last. Such a principle of living would indeed make a difference to things; obviously it would have a meaning and thereby justify its factual status according to the test of the logical positivist or the rabid empiricist.

It's another question, however, whether this interpretation of the Christian faith accords with what the New Testament teaches about the Faith. It is surely fair to argue that, since belief in a transcendent God and in what he has revealed about himself in the gospel is (according to the New Testament witness) the basis of our knowledge of Christian love as well as the only source of the requisite inspiration to practice it, such an interpretation as the above is alien to the faith proclaimed by early believers.

To confuse the Faith with an intention to live according to some high principle is to confuse it with law. But the trouble with the law, as set forth in the Bible, is its inability to supply the necessary power for men to carry out its commands. It's belief in the facts set forth in the gospel that makes the difference. (*How* they come to be known is another matter. What we are saying at the moment is simply this: it is the conviction that the Faith is dealing with *facts* that makes the difference.) For law, however "holy and just and good" (Romans 7:12), isn't equipped to meet man's weakness any more than a mirror, which can most efficiently reflect a dirty face, can be used to wash it.

The believer should certainly welcome every honest effort at analyzing the language of faith in order to try to make it as clear as humanly possible. We don't have the impression that the early witnesses to the good news wished to hide their message behind a curtain of verbosity when they called the world to faith. The facts they proclaimed didn't need the support of mumbo-jumbo to protect faith from probes into its meaning. Those witnesses were neither crackpots nor shrinking-violet types, as the Apostle Paul pointed out to the Roman Governor (Acts 26:25, 26). They well knew the reality of what they taught. Moreover, the believer is encouraged to learn wisdom from whatever source it may come. To the extent that the skeptic serves to discourage wild flights into the spiritual stratosphere, he may well be a divine rod meant to chasten undisciplined theologians. To change the metaphor: a logic that cleans the milk bottles should be welcome, but when the process entails smashing them, little wonder that it becomes suspect. It strongly suggests that its cleaning process is really a device to get rid of the milk.

A PSYCHOLOGICAL ATTACK: FAITH EXPLAINS NOTHING

The attempt to slay faith with logic was doomed to failure for a number of reasons. Suffice it for our purpose to note what has often been pointed out — that the weapon used by the skeptic actually boomeranged on himself. For if the only statements that make sense are those which can be tested by the senses, how can the statement that says *this* have meaning, seeing that it is about a principle of thinking, not an observation of fact? When the logical positivist argues for his principle, aren't we witnessing another example of a man sawing off the branch on which he is sitting?

But if logic can't dispose of the meaningfulness of the propositions of the faith without itself committing suicide, let no one imagine that the battle for faith is over. For the same passion that created the ill-fated logical weapon also hit upon a psychological one. And this really cuts deeper, because unbelief has its roots more in the psyche than in the intellect. Thus, the revised argument runs, even if the word *God* may in theory have meaning, in fact it is destined to die, in Prof. Antony Flew's words, "a death by a thousand qualifications."[4] That is, you have to qualify what you mean by the love of God, for example, so much that you may as well give up.

What the skeptic is after in putting forward this argument will become clearer if we record at this point the substance of a parable[5] which has had a good run in the trade, but which may not be so familiar to the layman who isn't versed in philosophical theology. The parable itself originally came from Prof. John Wisdom in the form of a tale; it was adopted by Flew to show how the meaning of theological statements disappears from view more and more as you continue to ask questions about them. The tale is about two men who come across a clearing in a jungle. Both flowers and weeds grow in the clearing, and an argument is started between the two explorers when one says that a gardener must be tending the plot. The other thinks not. So they decide to settle the matter by pitching their tents and watching. As no one ever turns up, it is suggested by the "Believer" that he may be an invisible gardener. In case that might be true, a fence is set up and electrified. Bloodhounds are also used, in case the gardener might be capable of being smelled though he couldn't be seen (like H. G. Wells's Invisible Man). Yet nothing ever happens to give grounds for believing that anyone was visiting the plot. "Yet still the Believer isn't convinced," we're told. He still holds that "there is a gardener who comes secretly to look after the garden which he loves." At last the Skeptic despairs and asks the Believer, "But what remains of your original assertion? Just how does what you call an invisible, intangible, eternally elusive gardener differ from an imaginary gardener or even from no gardener at all?"

ATTACKS BASED ON A SUPERFICIAL VIEW OF FACT

Thus we are once more confronted with the question asked earlier in this chapter: how would facts be different if there were no God? In other words, if atheism were true, what kind of world would this be? Illustrations are, of course, notoriously dangerous, for they are frequently used as if they were *proving* some point, when in fact they may simply be clarifying it.

A second look at the parable will show how deceptive it is when used by the opponent of faith to empty the believer's contention of meaning. For one thing, it assumes that an invisible gardener is essentially parallel to an invisible God. Now we would all agree that the Believer in the parable is obviously being stupid. Indeed, it takes a story to invent him, for we all know that there are no such gardeners as the Believer is looking for. All the gardeners we know have to handle visible and tangible materials with hands which also have sense properties. But the God of the Christian faith is held to be the reality *behind* all sense objects, as their *origin,* not as one of them. But there is nothing about sense objects as such that tells us they alone can be real. Hence, to argue that he who created the world and upholds it must be like it in space and time, if he is to have any meaning, is to assume the very thing that has to be proved. And the parable in question does just that.

Belief in an invisible power that accounts for the visible world is *not* patently absurd (as was the gardener), as the history of thought, together with common sense, attests. Multitudes of perfectly sane people have reflected on the world in which they found themselves and concluded that it was dependent on something other than itself for existence. To anyone who has clearly grasped this, one thing that would be different if there were no God is that there would be no world either.

The skeptic assumes that facts must always be of the same order as events that can be recorded or objects that can be photographed. But there are other facts of a different character, which have a power of their own. I mean those dynamic facts that have to do with the inner life of man, with the deep issues of life's purpose and destiny, and the experiences that evoke in man the sense of the holy and lead him to worship. That these facts aren't private fancies of the individual, but experiences which can be shared among vast numbers (as sense experiences can be shared among those whose senses operate normally) must surely cause one to ponder about the ultimate meaning of "fact."

If facts are just what one can experience as a spectator, it isn't given to anyone to explain *why* the world should be as we find it, rather than otherwise, from the standpoint of *how* it works. If you ask *why* it works, the exterior facts won't supply the answer. The arrangement of the wheels of a watch don't tell us who made it. Laplace, the astronomer, didn't need to bring God into the picture in order to ascertain the behavior of the heavenly bodies. But Laplace the *man* couldn't be satisfied without belief in God, and he knew this. No man is solely identifiable with his trade or profession. We may be sure that the epitaph on a successful businessman's tombstone, "Born a man and died a grocer," wasn't meant as a compliment.

The question whether life is "a tale told by an idiot, full of sound and fury, signifying nothing" arises from those hidden springs within, which have dynamic power in man's thinking and in his reaction to life and the world around. It was said of an aristocrat in an automobile that, having lost his way, he also lost his temper with a country yokel. To questions about the way and distance to the nearest town, the latter could only answer, "I don't know, sir." To the irate motorist's final question, "Is there anything you *do* know?" came the retort, "I know, sir, that I ain't lost!"

The present fashion is to regard as meaningless the question whether life has a purpose or meaning. This betrays how the popular view of what constitutes fact in philosophical circles today is dominated by "the despotism of the eye." The trend isn't new. A similar mentality lay behind what St. Paul called "the worship of the creature more than the Creator." The consequences of the resultant void are serious and tragic, as the destructive effects of modern attempts at finding substitutes for true fulfillment clearly indicate. And it is surely significant that many have actually come to faith through the failure of the sense world to answer the questions which nature herself prompts within a man, thus completely reversing in practical life the academic arguments of the skeptic. And to say, as Moritz Schlick does, that "there is no unfathomable mystery in the world" is itself to place one's faith in a theory concerning the ultimate meaninglessness of facts, rather than in facts themselves, which quite obviously cannot tell us whether or not they have meaning.

WHAT DETERMINES OUR VIEW OF FACT

What needs to be realized, then, is that what a man gets out of the facts will depend on the way he looks at them. If he decides beforehand that he will accept only the deliverances of his five senses and of logic, he will fail to see large areas of life that otherwise would have something significant to teach him. Thus a man's *interests* play a decisive part in the way he comes to see what is meaningful and what isn't. His interests determine the objects of his serious attention and act as blinders to the range of his vision. In one of his essays, Father Ronald Knox said of an argument he was examining that it appealed to him about as much as the last catalog on baby linen sent to him in the mail! We understand that such a catalog would be of little interest to him and he would have discarded it immediately, no matter how attractively it might have been produced. But to a mother of a newborn baby, it might have been meaningful because of its relevance to her needs.

If I say that the Prodigal Son's elder brother worked on his father's farm but didn't live in the same world as his father,

I'm guilty of blatant contradiction — unless it is appreciated that I'm making a distinction between the world of space, on the one hand, and that of spirit, on the other. And just as a historian has to select for study those facts that seem to him relevant for his particular interest, so the person who is interested only in the world of space and time — the world of the senses — will inevitably be tempted to conclude that everything else is a creation of prejudice or fancy.

What we have just argued is illustrated clearly in a work by Madden and Hare,[6] who quite openly declare that they aren't at all excited about souls being formed or people becoming righteous. To them, therefore, those issues we have mentioned about the inner life of man are irrelevant in considering the fact of God and the authenticity of faith. But to the believer these factors provide the most significant clue to the nature and meaning of things. It is these facts that enabled Job to see his sufferings in a light that made a difference to him. "When he has tried me," he said, "I shall come forth as gold" (Job 23: 10, KJV). So belief in God, which wouldn't make sense to a spectator (like the skeptic in Flew's parable), is full of meaning to one whose access to him isn't through things that can be weighed and measured.

I recall a bishop once saying how, as a curate, he used to visit his parishioners on a bicycle. It was a depressing task to have to push his bicycle up the hills, but what a difference it made when he got a motorcycle (what he called a "spirit-filled bike"). The hills were still there, but they were no longer obstacles. The man facing them was different.

If God is Spirit, to expect a description of him in sense terms would be absurd. So Yuri Gagarin, like the Skeptic in the parable, could have his little joke in reporting that his flight into space had supplied further evidence that no God was up there. Spiritual things are spiritually discerned, as the apostle says. To demand sense evidence before coming to faith is "to kick up dust and then complain that we cannot see." Gazing at the world outside, without appropriating the truth of Christ within, won't take us very far along the road to faith. What if it is so ordained that all the "furniture of heaven and earth" will not speak of God to the person who has no real interest in him? God is never on show to the curious. "You will find me," it is written, "when you seek me with all your heart" (Jeremiah 29:13). And didn't the Author of the believer's faith make it clear that it was the pure in heart, not the nimble of mind, who would see God? Hence, the most real fact of all may also be the most elusive.

I have sought to show how the perception of meaning is largely determined by interest, and how interest, in turn, awakens the attention to what before seemed remote and unreal. We can appreciate how the Skeptic in the parable became exasperated, for if any gardener were to be perceived at all, it was taken for granted that he would be witnessed by the senses. And, as we have seen, the parable assumes that God likewise, if he is real, can only be known in the same way. The parable, then, doesn't face the fact that the real is far greater than what can be defined in sense terms and, consequently, than what can be experienced by the senses.

WHY THE MEANING OF LIFE IS SO IMPORTANT

But the parable in question doesn't take another fact into account. It is the question of what happens *ultimately*. Nothing arises more spontaneously from man's nature than the question about life's meaning. What is it all about? Where does it lead? Death seems to be an intruder. Why should it cause man to ponder if he is fundamentally one with the dust of the ground? Human nature, like material nature, abhors a vacuum. We are not, incidentally, referring to the desire for "pie in the sky when you die," although it's interesting to observe how many who despise the longing for pie in the next world aren't loath to give it primary consideration in this life. We are thinking rather of the necessity of taking seriously the destination of life if we are to grasp its nature. For if to be shoveled underground or scattered on its surface is the end of the journey, then life in the last analysis is a mere passing show without meaning, which no amount of dedication or sacrifice can redeem. In other words, the future illumines the present; what a thing becomes reveals what it is.

My contention is, then, that any definition of meaning that

rules out consideration of *ultimate* meaning must be partial and arbitrary. The evaluation of the significance of life, moreover, cannot but affect one's response to its obligations. No theological sophistry or philosophical gymnastics can erase the question so deeply engraved within: "If a man die shall he live again?" We have said that St. Paul frankly admits that "if in this life only we have hoped in Christ, we are of all men most to be pitied" (1 Corinthians 15:19). And as no one has been raised to such heights of hope as the believer, no one could suffer so shattering a downfall if it were true that faith is just nonsense. For faith claims to have seen through the transience of the visible and caught a glimpse of the eternity of things not seen.

Now you will notice that Professor Flew makes the Skeptic in the parable represent the gardener not only as invisible, but also as "eternally elusive." What justifies the leap from what is elusive for a given period of time to what must be elusive eternally? Doesn't the New Testament refer to the distinction between a faith that will give up after a while and one that "endures to the end"? (Matthew 10:22). In fact it explicitly reminds us that God's time is not ours. "With the Lord one day is as a thousand years, and a thousand years as one day" (2 Peter 3:8). And if it is true that God had in mind an eternal purpose for man when he made him in his own image, doesn't our present existence become a mere drop in the endless ocean of the divine life? Let's suppose a child had been taken to the beach for the first time and that he plays in the sand for a few hours while the tide is coming in, but is taken home before the tide turns. Wouldn't it be understandable if the child should imagine that the tide would continue to flow until it covered the whole land? For he had no experience at all of the turn of the tide. And if he happened to be a rather precocious child, he would even argue that if the laws of nature were uniform, the sea would have to behave in the future as he had experienced it behaving in the past. Yet his conclusion would be false, being based on too limited a knowledge of the facts.

It is the prevailing bias towards the space-time dimension, then, that dictates the belief that faith is nonsense. Since man assumes that what isn't sense doesn't make sense, he can't trust himself out of his own sight. And having become, as he thinks, the measure of all things, he can see nothing that makes a great and unconditional demand upon him, which at the same time can lift him up to heights yet unrealized though eternally purposed for him. For this reason, the skeptic cuts himself off from proving the reality of what the apostle described as being "raised together with Christ," and from seeing how "this slight momentary affliction is preparing for us an eternal weight of glory beyond all comparison" (2 Corinthians 4:17).

BRINGING FAITH "UP TO DATE"

But even if all agreed that the charge, "Faith in God doesn't make sense," can't be sustained, we would still have to face a second, more subtle assault on faith — from the direction of those who themselves don the Christian uniform. I have in mind writers who believe that the traditional belief in a God who is beyond and behind the world is now out of date. God in fact isn't a being beyond the world at all, but, as Wren-Lewis puts it, "a supreme value which can actually be realized in ordinary experience." According to this view, then, a *personal* Being isn't the truth to stress, but a supreme *value*. The question that will occupy our attention to the end of this chapter is whether the substitution of personal values for a personal God affects faith in the Christian sense of the word. Or is it that, even though both are retained in theory, the shift of emphasis from one to the other is fatal for faith, and tantamount to denying the Christian message?

The difficulty of representing God in human terms has been with us from the beginning of man's spiritual pilgrimage. And because God is a unique fact, rather than simply an immense enlargement of the human species, it has generally been conceded that nothing we say of God in finite terms can be literally true. Thus, when we speak of him as a Father in heaven, we are really using picture language, an analogy, not a literal representation; for we don't wish to imply that we believe in a being who occupies, together with his family, a spot in space located somewhere high above the world. The temptation of falling into anthropomorphism — of imagining God after the form of human being — has led some to the conviction that we may speak of God legitimately only by saying what he is *not*. Others, however, hold that the only appropriate response to him is worship in silence, since all speech about him must of necessity distort the truth.[7]

The warning against thinking of God too much in human terms is in line with the biblical revelation of God. Thus, the prophet Isaiah is told to address his nation in God's name with the solemn challenge: "To whom then will ye liken me, that I should be equal to him? said the Holy One . . . Hast thou not known? hast thou not heard? the everlasting God, the Lord, the Creator of the ends of the earth, fainteth not, neither is weary; there is no searching of his understanding" (Isaiah 40:25, 28, KJV). St. Paul also tells us that "no one comprehends the thoughts of God except the Spirit of God" (1 Corinthians 2:11). And Christ himself declared that "no one knows the Father except the Son and any one to whom the Son chooses to reveal him" (Matthew 11:27).

THE BANISHMENT OF GOD

The view we are now considering, however, isn't content with shunning anthropomorphism. It's not a question of pruning the Faith of alleged accretions or of mythological expressions now out of date. The desire today is far more revolutionary and radical. In fact, an operation is called for that entails cutting out what has all along been held as the heart of faith. Nor is there any hope, it would appear, of transplantation. For this transcendent God himself must go — the one about whom we speak, not simply the way we speak of him.

Perhaps many will wonder what is supposed to be new about all this. Isn't it a case of plain atheism, which is as old almost as history? Didn't the "fool" say in his heart, in the days of the psalmist, that there is no God? The exponents of the view we are examining at present would be highly indignant at being classed with common or garden atheists or with those who deny the truth of Christianity. What Professor Braithwaite (a philosopher), Paul van Buren (a theologian), and John Wren-Lewis (a scientist), together with others who have been impressed by the arguments of the skeptic, are claiming is that the Christian faith must be translated into modern idiom, so that what is of real value in it may be applied to our own day. What interests us, as we have said, is whether in their keenness for the *modern* character of the idiom, they have forgotten the translation. In other words, are they saying to "modern" man what the gospel is saying? When one well-known cleric undertook a similar task a few years ago, he burned his fingers pretty badly. But some other writers on a similar theme give the impression that they have asbestos fingers and no inhibitions whatever in consuming the rubbish, theologically speaking, that long ago should have been committed to the flames.

The argument runs along these lines: modern science and logical method have abolished a transcendent God. The plain fact is that God is the potential for good within man himself. He is the way of love in human life, in short. "If we can say," writes John Wren-Lewis, "— as I believe we can — that love is indeed worthy of the name God, then it is possible to believe that the world can be so changed that ultimately all frustrations to personal life can be overcome, even death itself. This was exactly what the first Christians did believe . . ."[8] He even goes as far as to say that such love may "perhaps even . . . give new life to those who have died." So what is new here, what old-fashion atheism didn't claim, is that authentic Christian faith can preserve its identity without the God we have always thought existed as an independent being beyond the world of nature and men.

One cannot but feel that the words just quoted make strange reading after their author has described the unbelievably credulous religion of his mother, with its notion of occult realities behind the scenes. For all we know, his criticism of his mother's religion may be perfectly justified. Indeed, we aren't in the least interested in preserving anything that needs jettisoning in our own particular tradition. Our Lord came down heavily on the idea that the punctilious observance of traditional ritual and creeds could be a substitute for the truth. Even so, it would be difficult to conceive of anything which better illustrated the occult than the confession of faith in the passage just cited. And if that faith is true, there must be a good deal more behind the scenes than even our innocent forefathers suspected. Indeed, whatever myths traditional Christianity has in the past believed as literal facts, I doubt whether those myths were more out of touch with the facts of modern science, or of modern man, than the belief that human love may be able to render the human body incorruptible.

THE WEAKNESS OF "MODERN" FAITH

Is the substitute offered for a transcendent God in line with the essential meaning of the Faith? My contention is that it is not.

In the first place, if faith, instead of trust in God, becomes confidence in the human potential, prayer becomes soliloquy. It will be simply a case of man talking to himself. And however profitable self-meditation may be, it is surely different from addressing another, and what is more important, from being addressed by him. The profoundest purpose of prayer is to be in fellowship with *God,* not with ourselves — not even with ourselves in the depth of our being. The deeper down we go into the self, the less justification we have for thinking that we have a right to trust in ourselves.

Man's curse is fundamentally his self-centeredness, and fellowship simply with others like himself cannot deliver him from his egocentric predicament. The substitute for the transcendent God now offered to us, in hopes of avoiding the anthropomorphic pit, paradoxically hurls us into anthropocentrism. Man from now on must occupy the center. But that has been his trouble from the first, when he went astray in order to go his own way, which turned out to be the way of corruption, the way of spiritual death.

Second, the "translation" of the transcendent into the immanent must of necessity change the color of sin, which can no longer be "exceeding sinful." It means that the gospel is a technique for research rather than a call to repentance. Sin is no longer an offense against a holy God, but an injudicious treatment of oneself and one's neighbors. Such a do-it-yourself salvation forfeits the very thing Christ came to give the world: that freedom which is freedom indeed (John 8:36), the most dynamic fact man can ever know.

Third, what has this "translation" done with Christian hope? Evidently, there is very little good news in it. At best it is purely hypothetical, whereas at worst it is positively unjust. It is sheer hypothesis because it is prefaced by a very big *if*: "If we can say . . . that love is worthy of the name God . . . then it is possible. . . ." The author of those words is expressing a hoping-for-the-best type of faith, not the faith based, as Christian faith claims to be, on a finished and final fact. There is no "perhaps" in the teaching of Christ, not because he was more dogmatic than the rest of us, but because truth is sacred and secure. Hypotheses, however attractive, are not. "Fear not, little flock," he said, "for it is your Father's good pleasure to give you the kingdom" (Luke 12:32). And, "Because I live, you will live also" (John 14:19). This is echoed with the same assurance, because it is based on accomplished fact, by the Apostle Paul: "The Lord Jesus Christ will change our lowly body to be like his glorious body, by the power which enables him even to subject all things to himself" (Philippians 3:20, 21).

The substitute hope, however, is unjust. The countless multitudes who will have contributed to the hypothetical Utopia of the future are not to have any share in the fruit of their labor. But if they are to share this fruit, then the Faith which affirms that this can be so only by the power of an almighty God surely strains reason far less than faith in man's potential does. In any case, the *Christian* faith teaches unambiguously that death is a certainty, but that the "second death," not the dissolution of this physical frame, is the most serious in its consequences. "It is appointed for man to die once, and after that comes judgment" (Hebrews 9:27).

Finally, we are obliged to ask: "Where is this all-transforming love to be located?" How can man derive it from within himself? Christian faith does not pretend to rely on man's own possibilities. Only the Spirit of God — the God who is not to be equated with man — can bring breath into the "valley of dry bones," which is the human heart and human society without God. Man can act in this context only as he hears God himself speak and as he gratefully responds in humble faith. It is significant that Wren-Lewis converts the biblical "God is love" into the humanistic "love is God," and he even quotes the Apostle John in support of this. What John actually wrote was "love is *of* God" (1 John 4:7). We do not love of ourselves. "Herein is love, not that we loved God, but that he loved us, and sent his Son to be the propitiation for our sins" (1 John 4:10, KJV).

Of course, anyone can complain that multiplying texts proves nothing. But we are only interested here in pointing out that, according to what the Faith proclaimed in the Scriptures teaches, a God reduced to man-size is not the God of the gospel. The transcendent God alone can be a proper object of faith. The good news was precisely that the transcendent became immanent in the incarnation; that he through whom all things were made is the only power that can remake all things. Creation and redemption are therefore inseparable in the Christian faith. And the love that bore the cross also has the keys of death. The transcendence of the God of faith, consequently, is not the isolation of that God from our world. The proposition that "God must be understood," as Farrer remarks, "as a being about whom we have something to do"[9] could well be emended to "a being about whom we have *everything* to do," according to the Faith.

Is the Faith, then, out of date, and therefore to be avoided? The date on a thing doesn't indicate its truth and power. (No one objects to breathing because our remote forefathers did it so long ago.) Some things change with time, and other things don't. Battering rams are out of date, but war isn't. We shouldn't be too hasty about following the spirit of the age, for, as Dean Inge remarked, "He who marries the Spirit of the Age will soon find himself a widower." The Faith sets no store on obscurantism, so we must endeavor to distinguish between the various meanings of *out of date*. As for the present fashion of conducting God-funerals, we can recall the words of Athanasius: "Don't be alarmed, my children; for this is only a little cloud, and will quickly pass away."[10]

To conclude, let me say that however castigated as "meaningless" the God who is beyond the world may be, to demote him to merely human dimensions is to give him a "meaning" at the price of forfeiting his power. It is central in the Faith that he who gave Christ to the world is the eternal, invisible, and transcendent Spirit, the Alpha and the Omega of things seen and unseen. Any other "translation" is a travesty of the truth, the creation of "another gospel," and one that is no good news.

CHAPTER THREE

Reason Called to Witness

To grant that the word *God* has a meaning is one thing; to claim evidence for believing that there is a fact corresponding to it is another. Yet the question of God's actual existence is all-important. What we shall now attempt is to examine reason's witness in this matter.

We should be aware at the outset of certain complications that will inevitably arise in our quest. For one thing, the term *reason* is an umbrella under which even opposing schools of thought take shelter together. Second, it isn't always easy even for reason to keep a cool and clear head when engaged in so momentous an undertaking as our present inquiry involves. For in speaking of God and of faith we are dealing with ultimate issues whose effects on a man's life are beyond calculation. Little wonder, therefore, that Sir Alfred Ayer, in the second edition of *Language, Truth, and Logic,* should imply that some of his pronouncements in the first edition were due to the passion of youth. Yet passion is the last thing we expect of reason — unless she be prompted by desire and feeling disguised through the use of academic language.

But even though the journey may not be smooth, it may still have beneficial results. For it can teach us to appreciate to a greater degree the real nature of faith and the secret by which she lives. It may also help us to give due place to whatever light reason may shed on our path of inquiry, without permitting ourselves to be blinded by it.

A CLASH OF VIEWS ON THE PLACE OF REASON

When we ask whether faith can face the tests of reason or not, the response does not come, as we might have expected, from a detached and dignified figure who despises any taint of emotion when seeking to understand. For as soon as the question is raised, a babel of voices will be found shouting one another down and claiming to be doing so in the service of truth.

Take one or two examples from *the camp that regards reason as hostile to faith.* Thus, that fiery and forceful lawyer Tertullian (c. A.D. 160-220) comes down heavily on those philosophers who dare to enter the territory of faith with their all-important weapon — reason. He lambasts Aristotle for teaching a logic which was "self-stultifying, since it is ever handling questions but never settling anything." With his powerful rhetoric Tertullian then throws out the challenge: "What is there in common between Athens and Jerusalem? What between the Academy and the Church . . . after Christ Jesus we desire no subtle theories, no acute inquiries after the gospel."[1] And he calls Greek philosophy the bridal gift of fallen angels to the daughters of men.

Nearer to our own age we find the Scottish thinker David Hume (1711-1776) referring to "those dangerous friends, or disguised enemies of the Christian religion, who have undertaken to defend it by the principles of human reason. Our most holy religion is founded on Faith, not on reason; and it is a sure method of exposing it to put it to such a trial as it by no means is fitted to endure." Let us not be misled by such language into fancying that Hume was another Tertullian, joining the happy throng who wave the banner of the faithful. What makes his remarks interesting is that he doesn't really set out to champion faith, as Tertullian does, but to show how faith cannot stand the test of reason. For we notice that he speaks of the danger of "exposing" religion! Hume, unless I am doing him gross injustice, is writing with his tongue in his cheek. In any case, even if he spurned the use of reason to *defend* faith, he had no qualms about using it to throw doubt on faith.

In our own day we can look at what the Swiss theologian

Karl Barth has to say on the relation between reason and faith. To him our knowledge of God can only come to us "perpendicularly from above." It comes from God's sovereign grace and without any intention of consulting reason in the matter. Like everything else that is human, reason is "fallen." It is too weak and bruised to rise above the horizontal, earthly level to the dimension of the divine.

These are a few representatives of the camp that regards reason as hostile to faith. But we mustn't conclude from what has been said so far that all believers would jettison reason in matters that have to do with faith. On the contrary, reason has its friends within the circle of believers, quite a number of them. From the early Christian era, in fact, there have been those who have regarded Christ as "the reason of whom the whole human race partake." Clement of Alexandria (c. A.D. 200) wrote of philosophy (whose instrument is reason) as "the schoolmaster to bring the Greek mind to Christ as the law brought the Hebrews." Many others, including Anselm, Aquinas, Descartes, and Leibniz, ranged themselves with those who held the view that *reason and faith should be walking together* rather than be at each other's throats.

Before passing any opinion on what has been quoted, we may note another view of the relation between reason and faith. It comes from the camp that holds *reason to be not hostile, but incompetent to pronounce on faith.* Any attempt on reason's part to assess faith would only expose *reason,* and not, as Hume thought, expose faith. Let us hear what Martin Luther, for instance, has to say on the matter: "Would he not be a great fool, who in thick of battle sought to protect his helmet and sword with bare hand and unshielded head? It is not different when we essay with our reason to defend God's law, which should rather be our weapon."[2] Immanuel Kant, likewise, sought to establish the incompetence of reason to penetrate the realm of faith. He tells us that he had to drive out knowledge to make room for faith. This wasn't, however, a case of opting for ignorance. Rather, Kant was clipping the wings of reason to stop her flying beyond her legitimate limits. Indeed, when she forgot her limits Kant showed what a sorry figure she cut. And remembering what happened to

Icarus when he flew too near the sun and the wax in his wings melted, we are tempted to suspect that Kant was doing reason a service.

DIFFERENT TYPES OF REASON

What shall we conclude from this? No answer should be attempted without first considering the fact that "reason" doesn't always bear a uniform meaning. We sometimes speak of reasoning as the process of drawing logical conclusions from given premises. It takes the form of "if this is true, then that must follow." Such deductive reasoning is concerned only with the validity of the process of reasoning from premises to conclusion. It doesn't pretend to say whether the conclusion itself is true or false, for to know the truth of the conclusion, one would have to know the truth of the premises. We live in a world full of facts that logic is impotent to handle. It would be futile to ask a clever but blind logician to tell us whether there was, say, a crow on yonder tree. A five-year-old whose sight was sound would be a greater authority on such a matter.

The relevance of this point in the present discussion is clear. A logician, as such, has no special qualifications for either affirming or denying the existence of God. He might point out that a particular mode of reasoning about God's existence (or about his nonexistence) was illogical, but that wouldn't settle the question of the *truth* of the conclusion. And just as we can affirm conclusions, which are in fact not true, from a process of reasoning that is valid, so we also can come to true conclusions despite the invalidity of the process of reasoning. Thus, I may say that because all human beings have two legs and Chairman Mao has two legs, therefore Chairman Mao is a human being. The conclusion that Chairman Mao is a human being happens to be true, but it does not logically follow from my premises. Chickens also have two legs.

Reasoning in the purely logical sense of the word cannot prove God's existence. But neither can it establish the fact that we ourselves exist. So no one need lose sleep over this matter, seeing that such reasoning tells us more about the limits of logic than about any uncertainty over the existence of God.

We can understand what the medieval philosopher John of Salisbury meant when he said that experience had taught him "a manifest conclusion, that while logic furthers other studies, it is by itself lifeless and barren." (The reader can draw his own conclusions about the attempt of one celebrated thinker of the eleventh century, who thought he had found a sure way of proving God's existence by calling on logic to take a leading part in the task. This argument I shall outline presently.)

Meanwhile, let us see whether another kind of reasoning can bring us to a knowledge of God. This reasoning proceeds inductively. That is, it examines a number of facts at hand and seeks to draw what would appear to be "reasonable" conclusions from them. It will ask, for example, whether belief in God fits in with facts that we know from experience to be true. It tries to make sense of the world, for reason cannot stand a picture with blurred outlines, a pattern that is incoherent and incomplete. And some thinkers today, just as centuries ago, are convinced that a fair, rational, reflection on the facts of the world must lead any unbiased person to conclude that a creator made the world we know. "Reason," says F. H. Cleobury, "is not merely a break-down gang removing obstacles; it is a gang laying the track."[3] I believe that this conclusion is the natural one for those who already believe in God or who, at least, are disposed to believe.

Whether anyone can be really unprejudiced when discussing matters of such moment as the Christian faith, I very much doubt. Be that as it may, the point to be stressed here is that what is absurd to expect from reason in one sense of the word, may be legitimate to expect from reason in another sense. Rhetoric about the impotence of reason as such doesn't further the cause of faith. "If reason is understood as a blanket term for the sound functioning of our mental capacities, then one who attacks the competence of reason is committing himself not to the Church but to the asylum,"[4] one writer declares. However, we surely need to qualify that statement by reminding ourselves that areas of reality may well exist in which even reason in the inductive sense is out of her depth. In any case, to deify reason is as foolish as to despise it. Divorced from facts, which are themselves not discoverable by reason,

reason must lose her power. On the other hand, without reason, facts themselves lose their significance.

IMPORTANT DISTINCTIONS

Unless the different connotations of the term *reason* are kept in mind, we may unwittingly do injustice to pronouncements made on the witness of reason to faith. Thus, Martin Luther once wrote, "All the articles of Christian belief are, when considered rationally, impossible and mendacious and preposterous. Faith, however, is completely abreast of the situation. It grips reason by the throat, and strangles the beast." Karl Barth uttered a loud Amen to that statement by saying: "He who can hear this, let him hear it; for it is the beginning and end of history." To that remark Professor Paton reacts with the comment: "It sounds more like the end of human sanity."[5] I doubt, however, whether in this context Barth merits the stick so severely. For in a sense both Luther and Barth are echoing St. Paul's address to the Corinthians about the way God has "made foolish the wisdom of this world" (1 Corinthians 1:20), and that "the foolishness of God is wiser than men" (1 Corinthians 1:25). When Luther affirmed that all the articles of the Christian faith were preposterous, he surely meant that there was a *type* of reasoning that regarded them as such. In fact, we have already considered such "reasoning" riding high under the banner of logical positivism.

In support of this contention are Luther's words in another context: "Reason is light in this dwelling, and unless the Spirit, which is lighted with the brighter light of faith, controls this light of reason, it cannot but be in error."[6] And in his *Table-Talk* Luther remarks: "The understanding, through faith, receives life from faith; that which was dead is made alive again; like as our bodies, in light day when it is clear and bright, are better disposed, rise, move, walk, etc., more readily and safely than they do in the dark night, so it is with human reason, which strives not against faith when enlightened, but rather furthers and advances it."[7]

Another example that illustrates how the theological pitch is muddied by confining the meaning of some key words to a single sense, thereby loading the argument from the start, is found in Professor A. J. Ayer's statement of the case: "We are often told that the nature of God is a mystery which transcends the human understanding. But to say that something transcends the human understanding is to say that it is unintelligible. And what is unintelligible cannot significantly be described. . . . But if one allows that it is impossible to define God in intelligible terms then one is allowing that it is impossible for a sentence both to be significant and to be about God."[8]

In order to effect so summary a disposal of faith by a straightforward bit of logic, it was necessary to assume the very thing experience seems to deny; namely, that the terms *mystery, understanding, intelligible,* and *significant* have each only a single meaning. The fact is that in a sense everything is a mystery[9] which transcends the understanding. Let a child press his interminable whys? far enough, and the most penetrating logician will be glad of a break. The end of any path for mortal man is a mystery. It is not given to us to see very far. But we may fail to see either because we are looking into darkness or because we are looking into the blinding light of the sun. Mystery, likewise, may be due either to ignorance of the facts (hence mystery novels, mystery tours, etc.), or to the awareness of a reality whose splendor is more than our finitude can face.

Just as there are different types of reasoning, there are different types of seeing. We have said that it is possible to see how a conclusion must follow from certain premises. It is also possible to see the beauty of a humble spirit, but not by the same means as seeing a logical conclusion. We can also see a joke. To reduce all instances of seeing to a single category would be comic if it weren't so dangerous. It was said of one pundit, who had become obsessed with analysis of jokes, that he had discovered that only ten basic, genuine jokes existed. Thereafter, when he was told a joke, rather than laugh he would just say under his breath, "Yes, that is a joke," or the contrary. His obsession with the analytical approach to everything had let him down. Logic, likewise, can be a good servant but a bad master.

CAN REASON ASSESS REASON?

Another truth we must keep in mind in considering the witness of reason to faith is this: reason herself is conducting the inquiry. But what if the truth we seek to comprehend is outside reason's reach? Does that mean that such truth is neither relevant nor real for man? Does it mean *we* are outside *its* reach? By what logic can we say that such must be the case? A dime-store telescope can hardly be expected to tell us a great deal about the heavenly bodies in remote space. The limits of the owner's vision would tell us more about his telescope than about the stars. And what if he accused Professor Hoyle and Sir Bernard Lovell of fictionalizing instead of sticking to facts, on the grounds that his little instrument revealed no sign of the stars they were so enthusiastically talking about! Similarly, reason may prejudge the results of its inquiry by taking as axiomatic that what it cannot encompass must be nonexistent. St. Paul tells us that when "the Lord of glory" came into the world, not only did the religious establishment fail to see the glory, but they were blind to the fact that the defect was in themselves, not in Christ.

REASON'S ATTEMPTS AT FINDING GOD

A passing glance at how some thinkers have tried to discover God through reason will bring home to us how man is ever reaching out for something infinitely greater than his intellect can encompass. Detailed and full discussion of this field is so accessible to anyone interested that I don't propose to do more than illustrate a point or two in the present context. We may note, however, that the majority of contemporary writers on the classical arguments of reason for the existence of God no longer regard those arguments as proofs in the strict sense of the word, but as witnesses that eke out the deep-rooted conviction, held on other grounds, that God is an inescapable fact. In the case of the first two arguments below — which are examples of inductive reasoning — it is commonly supposed that they at least show the reasonableness of belief in God, while yet falling short of irrefutable demonstration.

One of these arguments (traditionally referred to as the

cosmological argument) seeks to show that the existence of a world such as the one we know requires an explanation. Our experience of "the way things are" teaches us that every effect has a cause. So the world is made up of a chain of causes and effects. From this it is argued that the world itself must have been caused by something or someone outside it. "What is more reasonable than that?" one may ask. But this argument invites awkward questions. Thus, there may be a system of cause and effect operating *within* the universe, but does this entail that the universe *itself* needs a cause from outside to explain it? Why cannot the universe have been in existence from eternity? Aristotle believed that it had always been there, and even Aquinas granted that reason was incapable of disproving this. He, however, believed that the world had been created, on the grounds that it had been made known by revelation. In any case, the question also arises whether it is legitimate to argue from a finite effect to an infinite cause. If you do this, doesn't your conclusion take you beyond what the premises warrant?

Another "proof" of God's existence is based on the seeming order and design exhibited by nature in such phenomena as the procession of the planets, the beauty of the world, and the astounding mechanism of the eye. But neither has this attempt (called the teleological argument) succeeded in dispelling all doubt concerning the need for a creator. There are patterns in nature which don't obviously require a mind to explain them, as, for example, when we say that Jack Frost has been at work overnight. But even if there is a mind behind nature, does the world of itself tell us that there is only *one* mind and that it must be omnipotent (such as faith affirms) rather than just very great?

To some thinkers, where the two above arguments have failed, what is known as the moral argument for God's existence succeeds. They are convinced that the possession of a moral sense, with its authoritative voice, is a clear witness to the existence of a lawgiver. On the other hand, it is argued that many who don't question the binding character of the moral law nonetheless don't believe in God. They are content to say that things are just like that and there is nothing else to it. But this is really throwing in the towel by refusing to allow that man can ever come to a knowledge of the truth. Others, while conceding that the arguments in question don't clinch the matter in a logical sense, maintain that there is such a thing as an illumination of the facts which reason cannot provide. Such illumination discloses to the one who reflects on the facts the finite nature of the world, including ourselves, and its dependence on a reality of another dimension. But this takes us to the borders of the territory of "religious experience," which we shall consider later.

Vexed at the thought that no foolproof argument for the existence of God had been discovered, Anselm, an Archbishop of Canterbury in the eleventh century, tells us how the answer came to him like a flash, just as he was on the point of despair. His "proof" proceeded thus: If you only consider the meaning of the word *God,* you will find that you cannot admit that you know what the word means and at the same time allow that he may not exist in reality. Now, Anselm takes it that you are on firm ground when you say that God is "that than which no greater can be conceived." He is not only that, but he is at least that. But such a God, who was only a thought in your head with no existence in reality, couldn't possibly be "one than which no greater can be conceived." For it is evident that a God who was both an idea within you *and* a fact outside you would be greater. Therefore, you cannot rationally say that you have the idea of such a God and then deny his existence. This attempt was later called the ontological argument.

Subtle and novel though the argument was, it didn't take long for a monk called Gaunilo to attack it with a criticism which amounted to saying that such a method of reasoning could prove almost anything. Thus, if I have in my head the idea of an island of such excellence and richness that no other island can be conceived to possess, then presumably I am obliged to affirm the real existence of that island! Anselm, however, soon sent the ball flying back into the monk's court. He pointed out that what Gaunilo had failed to see was that no island, or anything else that was a finite object, could possibly parallel the idea of an infinite being. Indeed, if Gaunilo could produce reasons for saying that his island was a fair parallel to "that than which no greater can be conceived," then Anselm would not only undertake to find that island but he would also make Gaunilo a present of it.

Anselm's "proof" met with little enthusiasm for centuries, but it was revived in a modified form by the seventeenth-century French thinker, René Descartes. A century later, however, Immanuel Kant set about demolishing it. He pointed out, for one thing, that an idea does not become any greater as an idea, if it happens to have something corresponding to it outside the mind. The idea of a five-dollar bill doesn't become the idea of more than five dollars just because you have such a bill in your wallet. Even so, the ghost of the ontological argument has haunted philosophers up to the present day. The reason for this is of primary interest for our present purpose, rather than the case made out for and against it. On the one hand, the argument as formulated seems to be too "clever" to be true. On the other hand, it seems to be inspired by something that cannot be other than true. That something is the conviction that the idea of God is unique.

Now, the uniqueness of the idea of God has important consequences with respect to how we come to knowledge of him. Anselm tells us that he isn't calling on reason to *find* faith, but rather to understand it. "I am not trying, O Lord, to penetrate thy loftiness, for I cannot begin to match my understanding with it, but I desire in some measure to understand thy truth, which my heart believes and loves. For I do not seek to understand in order to believe, but I believe in order to understand. For this too I believe, that 'unless I believe I shall not understand.' "[10]

THE LEGITIMACY AND LIMITATIONS OF REASON

Here, Anselm puts his finger on a truth we noted earlier: the failure of logical reasoning to prove God's existence must not be construed as implying that God is not there. It may be that God's "loftiness" (as Anselm calls it) is impenetrable to human reason. Even Kant, in seeking to show that reason couldn't prove God's existence, was keen on pointing out that it couldn't disprove it either. "Reason, for all the flourishing of her trumpets," wrote MacNeile Dixon, "has no greater success in illuminating the grand problems than the imagination. From the central keep of the world's mystery its arrows fall idly back, as from the walls of the medieval castle the bolts of the archer."[11] So though reason may not answer our perennial questions about the ultimate significance of life, "the craving that a ray of light may fall on the mystery of the existence of this world, or on the incomprehensible fact that it is comprehensible . . . even if such questions *could* be shown to lack a clear meaning . . . they are *not silenced.* There is something cheap in debunking them. The heart's unrest is not to be stilled by logic."[12]

Yet the alternative to refusing reason the last word in matters of faith is not the banishment of reason from this sphere, as we have seen. We cannot endorse without qualification Hume's representation of reason as the slave of the passions. As Gilson remarks, "Philosophy always buries its undertakers." Constructive reasoning may cohere significantly with faith, though faith may not be constructed out of reason. Faith is not the child of reason, but its twin. Life should be richer for both of them if they live together, seeing that they have the same Father.

At this point it would be well to recall the words of Pascal. "There are but two sorts of persons who deserve to be accounted reasonable; either those who serve God with all their heart because they know him, or those who seek him with all their heart, because they know him not."[13] Since we are by nature strangers and sojourners here; since we are recipients of life, not its creators, and are a surprise to ourselves; isn't it natural that we should seek the eternal Mystery? If there is a point at which reason must remain silent, as we have sought to show, that silence itself bears more eloquent witness to faith than all man's voluble speculations throughout the history of thought. To behave as though the understanding were supreme is to reveal a detachment, not from prejudice, but from truth. If man is to be rescued from the bog of meaninglessness and frustration, tugging at his own bootstraps will profit him nothing. Deliverance must come from another place. And that place is what faith is about.

CHAPTER FOUR

What About Science?

A physics master in an English grammar school, so it was reported, having concluded the required Scripture lesson, introduced the science period with the remark: "And now let us turn to something real." The popular notion that science has more or less superseded religion accounts for the great rejoicing in some religious circles whenever a scientist makes it known that he is a believer in the Christian faith. And to bolster up the status of faith, the names of famous scientists in the past, who were also believers, are often cited. Among the favorites are Galileo, Kepler, Descartes, Leibniz, Newton, and Pascal. That list could be supplemented by the names of many others, including notable contemporary scientists, who make no apology for their profession of Christianity.

WHY FAITH IS CONCERNED WITH SCIENCE

The question we shall consider in this chapter is why the rumor that science has discredited faith has gone abroad at all. What are the facts of the situation? We have already considered in broad outline the relation between reason and faith and the type of reasoning employed in logic and mathematics, together with other varieties of reasoning. But in what relation does *physical* science stand to the basic tenets of religion? If reason, when she claims absolute sovereignty, is a usurper in the realm of truth, have the physical sciences any greater authority to claim the seat of power? Or, as Farrer puts it, "Are we any wiser when we elevate physics into the throne from which we have pulled mathematics down? Is she queen of knowledge? Must all other claimants to factual truth . . . be judged by their likeness to the royal face?"[1]

That men of faith should be concerned with what science teaches is understandable, when we consider how many take science to be synonymous with certainty. To say "science has shown" is regarded as the last word on a matter, because it is held that science is only interested in facts. It has no private ax to grind. The truth, the whole truth, and nothing but the truth is its motto. Any faith, therefore, which purports to be keen on sticking to facts, will naturally want to know what science is telling the world. For if the pronouncements of science contradict the fundamentals of faith, someone obviously has to quit.

But why should it be thought that one must choose between science and faith? That question, to many, is easy. Hasn't the scientist, in whichever direction he has turned his eyes, shown quite categorically that religion has all along been romancing? When he looked upward to discover the facts, he found that the sun, not the earth, was the center around which the planets revolved. Hadn't the Church taught otherwise and made Galileo pay for daring to contradict? When the scientist looked down to the soil and rocks, he found that untold ages had passed before man appeared on the scene. Doesn't this contradict Holy Writ? When he looked around and examined the world of life in nature, he found an evolutionary process operating which, he believed, dispensed altogether with the need for a creator. And when he looked within, instead of finding an immortal soul, he discovered a menagerie where the snake and tiger and fox, and other animal instincts as yet untamed, were raging. Where, then, is the much publicized divine image? Doesn't it look as though the Bible is wrong again, and that instead of man having been made in the image of God, it was God who had been made in the image of man?

Such answers looked more impressive than they actually had a right to be; I hope presently to show why this is so. Suffice it at this point to note two facts. First, it isn't legitimate to equate the essential bases of genuine religious faith with what certain sections of the Church have pronounced at some time or other on particular issues about the world. Second, it is necessary to distinguish between (a) the undisputed facts which have been brought to light by science and (b) the philosophical (or theological) interpretation of those facts by particular scientists. In other words, a great difference exists between science and what may be called "scientism" — by which we mean the theories of a scientist who is wearing spectacles with philosophically-tinted lenses. Examples of scientism abound and we shall consider some of them here.

That fools rush in where angels fear to tread can be illustrated from the numerous dogmatic pronouncements of both scientists and religious people. What was written a decade ago about facile interpretations is still true, and just as true of clerics as of others. P. W. Kent stated that "the tendency to believe that the latest piece of opinion, hot from the press, is more likely to be right than that of a week ago is strongly to be deplored. Attempts to reconcile theological or philosophical questions with scientific advances before science itself has found its perspective, leads readily to those remarkable publications which are unhelpful at their inception, absurd within five years, and comic after ten."[2] A case in point was Aldous Huxley's statement in a magazine article, "Modern Science makes it impossible to believe in a personal God." Matching this is Freud's conclusion that "religion is a childhood neurosis." Nor is Bertrand Russell to be outdone in the practice of scientism, despite his erudition and genius as a scientist, as we shall see. Ernan Mullin likewise makes this point: "The tension is due to two main factors — the past efforts of theologians to regiment science and to extend their competence beyond its proper limits, and the growing 'Caesarism' of science, which seems to explain everything and to make supernatural modes of thought appear hopelessly old-fashioned."[3] Mullin concludes that "science has unquestionably encouraged the spread of irreligion." But, as we have said, strictly speaking it isn't *science* that is to blame.

Many well-meaning people have sought to solve the question of the relation between science and religion. Few can settle the matter at a stroke in the manner of Sir Alfred Ayer: "Since the religious utterances of the theist are not genuine propositions at all, they cannot stand in any logical relation to science."[4] The difficulty here, however, is that anyone in this world who responds to the call of faith, and yet wishes to stay here, must tear himself in two. The only alternatives would be either to renounce faith or to depart this life, seeing that no rational person would wish to be a Dr. Jekyll in religion and a Mr. Hyde in science. The believer cannot possibly rest in a position that regards the world perceived by the senses, on the one hand, and the God known by faith, on the other, as having no rational connection with each other. It is no doubt true that when faith affirms that the world was made by God, it doesn't imply that God makes things *as man does.* For science, to "explain" something is to relate it in some way to other things in the space-time dimension. Now, God isn't just another item of that nature. Even so, when we say that God made the world, we aren't uttering sounds without any sense. Rather, we are making a rational statement about the world's absolute dependence upon the creator for its existence and its persistence. "His invisible attributes, that is to say his everlasting power and deity, have been visible, ever since the world began, to the eye of reason, in the things he has made" (Romans 1:20, NEB).

ATTEMPTS TO RELATE FAITH AND SCIENCE

Various attempts have been made to relate religion and science within one universe. For example, it is said that both deal with facts, but not with the same type of facts: science concerns itself with things seen, and religion with things not seen, the former being material and the latter spiritual. But some scientists hold that this dichotomy can no longer be sustained, now that science has found a way of constructing "mind" out of material substances. John Habgood opens an article entitled "Minds and Machines,"[5] with this sentence, " 'I want you to meet Horace,' said the engineer. 'There is virtually no difference between him and a human being.' " Horace was a computer, but the engineer went on to show how "he" could make real decisions, learn from experience, and understand.

The engineer even apologized to Horace with "I was only joking" after the computer had shown by a green light that he was taking a dim view of being accused of pride! But long before scientists had claimed to have made mind out of matter in the shape of a computer, man had noticed that there was *some* obvious vital connection between the mental and the physical. If you hit a man with a crowbar in the right place, there will be no more spirit left in him.

Although the engineer's terminology when speaking of Horace was "loaded" and very loosely employed, the *apparent* inseparability of the spiritual from the physical (and consequently the suspicion that the former was only the latter in a complicated guise) has made a deep impression. Escape from materialism was then sought by apportioning to science the "know-how" and to faith the "know-why." But the materialistic scientist won't allow this. For him *why* and *what* are interchangeable. Thus, if you ask why a wooden log floats in water, you need only answer in terms of *what* in detail takes place, and everyone is satisfied.

Of course, if you want to be perverse, and go on to ask why should things be what they are and why should there be anything at all, modern philosophers leap to the aid of the scientist and say that your question doesn't make sense. We've already shown why this is so — namely, because only the explanations in terms of the sense world are allowed to qualify as sensible.

Another attempt to allot science and faith their respective kingdoms takes the form of a distinction between facts and values: science is the discipline that deals with the world of facts — religion, with the world of values (such as right and wrong, the good and the wicked). But this manner of dealing with the question isn't satisfactory either. For one thing, it's common to argue these days that the acknowledgement of values doesn't need religious sanction at all. The materialist, it is said, can be as conscientious in the matter of right and wrong as the so-called saints of religion. And yet he remains a materialist, being convinced that matter has the last word as well as the first.

WHY SCIENCE SEEMS TO THREATEN FAITH

Some people imagined that the clash between science and religion was settled when the Church accepted the theory of evolution and ceased to interpret everything in the Bible literally. But their optimism was short-lived. The atheist wasn't going to be placated with so meager a concession as that.

Lately it has become more apparent that the man of religion who magnanimously allows an unlimited length of rope to the scientist need not be surprised if he finds himself hanging by it. The suspicion persists that one or the other will have to assume overall sovereignty. Nor is this just the imagination of the faithful. Recent research in genetics, together with the ready manner in which sociologists and politicians and others have suggested how those findings should be put to practical use, have given good grounds to the religious for seeing a takeover on behalf of science in the making. And they can see looming on the not-so-distant horizon a "loftier" race, with the "light of knowledge in its eyes" — but with spiritual darkness in its heart.

Let us look briefly at some further reasons for the seeming threat of science to faith, and vice versa. First, both (through certain of their spokesmen) give the impression that they are dyed-in-the-wool *totalitarians*. They demand all or nothing. Anything less than all, apparently, would wreck their whole program. So it's of little use to try the panacea of "dialogue" in this matter. Let first the science camp speak out: "The scientist tries to rid himself of all faiths and beliefs. He either knows or he does not know. If he knows, there is no room for faith. If he does not know, he has no right to faith or belief." Or: "The goal of science is clear — it is nothing short of complete interpretation of the universe." Or: "Science does much more than demand that it shall be left in undisturbed possession of what the theologian and metaphysician please to term its 'legitimate field.' It asserts that the scientific method is the sole gateway to the whole region of knowledge."[6] In other words (with apologies to Cowper), the scientist is monarch of all he surveys, whose right there is none to dispute.

But neither is authentic faith disposed to compromise, any more than science. For its existence hangs on the reality of the Alpha and Omega of all things (1 Corinthians 15:28). Let science deride, if it must, all ultimate mystery; faith lives by it and revels in it. It quite openly marvels at "the depth of the riches both of the wisdom and knowledge of God! How unsearchable," it exults, "are his judgments, and his ways past finding out" (Romans 11:33, KJV).

Second, science and religion seem to clash in their *views of authority.* To the scientist, blind belief and unqualified trust are anathema. The men of religion who throw up to him the argument that science too exercises faith in entertaining hypotheses show that they are out of touch. For the scientist regards faith as a mere servant of sight, a kind of scout sent to view the possibilities ahead. Only when sight arrives on the scene does it possess the land. Hypotheses must go, if facts aren't forthcoming. But for men of religion, faith has a different status altogether. It is "the *assurance* of things hoped for, the conviction of things not seen" (Hebrews 11:1). Hasn't the man of faith often made it clear that entire submission to God's will is a mark of intellectual humility? For the scientist, on the other hand, real humility is willingness to learn from facts, and the function of the intellect is to ascertain these.

Third, don't science and religion have a different doctrine about the *correct method* for discovering truth? The scientist proceeds by observation and experiment. Prejudices must be set aside and private wishes must not be allowed to "cook" the results of the inquiry. But faith makes no attempt at concealing its desires. It longs to participate in the object of its search. It declares that God is its "refuge and strength, a very present help in trouble." Can anyone trust a man in such a frame of mind to carry out an objective inquiry? Won't he be tempted to read in, rather than "read off," when interpreting facts?

As for the experimental method, the scientist seems to regard everything as fair game. Curiosity rules the roost. The mentality that could forbid a team of mountaineers to set foot on a certain peak in the Himalayas because it was the sacred abode of the gods, would spell death to science. At least, so it would appear. But for faith, the very thought of defiled man daring to peer into the Holy of Holies, let alone to experiment with it, is profanity of the first order. Is godly fear, then, just an antique? Having lost its hold through the onward march of science, has it been reduced to the quaint?

Fourth, a clash between science and religion seems inevitable when one considers the totally different answers they seem to give to the question, "What is the significance of the world?" In other words, they hold opposing *metaphysical views* of the world. We have already seen how some have spoken quite dogmatically in the name of science, about religious faith: how one said that a personal God is "out"; how another spoke of religion as though it were simply a device for the toddler, so to speak. And the other day a member of a television panel declared she couldn't believe in God because she was a biologist. We can appreciate, therefore, why the term *scientist* is enough to arouse suspicion in some religious circles. The household of faith appears to be threatened by an enemy that won't be satisfied until it has scattered them for good.

We may cite another such pronouncement from the pen of Bertrand Russell. "That man is the product of causes which had no prevision of the end they were achieving; that his origin, his growth, his hopes, his fears, his loves and beliefs, are but the outcome of accidental collocation of atoms; . . . that all the labors of the ages . . . are destined to extinction in the vast death of the solar system . . . if not quite beyond dispute, are yet so nearly certain, that no philosophy which rejects them can hope to stand. Only within the scaffolding of these truths, only on the firm foundation of unyielding despair, can the soul's habitation henceforth be safely built."[7] When we set this statement by Russell side by side with the pronouncements of the New Testament, we cannot be left in any doubt about the infinite gulf that separates scientism from faith. Christ reassured his disciples just before his death that there would be a reunion later: "I go to prepare a place for you," was the promise, "that where I am you may be also" (John 14: 2, 3). Paul affirmed this: "Death is swallowed up in victory" (1 Corinthians 15:54). "We know that if the earthly tent we live in is destroyed, we have a building of God, . . . eternal in the heavens" (2 Corinthians 5:1-5).

Our question is: Are we to explain one of these pictures

about the future and about the meaning of our existence as based upon fact and the other as an expression of fancy?

THE PRESTIGE OF SCIENCE

Before we examine the position we have outlined, we may ask: "On what grounds is it so generally assumed that the scientist knows what he is talking about, while men of faith appear to be champions of fantasy?" The answer may become clear if we consider three facts. First, the findings of science are frequently relevant to our physical comfort. So, since the things nearest our heart are the things we regard as most real, we take it for granted that science always moves in the realm of indisputable fact. Second, the scientist has produced such "wonders" that we tend to ascribe potential omniscience to him; hence the sense of awe, almost, that his name evokes. Third, the statements of the scientist are open to investigation and verification, as, for instance, when a forthcoming eclipse is announced and described. From these three standpoints, then, you know where you are with science. It remains to be seen whether faith can stand up to similar considerations.

The success of science speaks for itself. But how does faith fare? Isn't it true that, far from catering to our physical comfort, faith warns against too much of it, and even exalts self-denial? No wonder it has been said that some people have just enough Christianity to make them miserable. Further, faith is commonly regarded as irrelevant to facts. Penicillin effects cures, but faith-healing is looked upon as the consolation of the credulous. Nor can you check up on the promises of faith as you can on the predictions of science. Saints may be perceptive enough to see blessings in disguise, but most people have to be content with seeing the disguise only. The faithful may find inspiration in singing, "Far off I see the goal," but the majority of the sons of Adam can't pretend to see that far.

THE FALLACIES OF PSEUDO-SCIENCE

We have already observed that we add to our confusion if we don't keep in mind the all-important distinction between scientism and science. The former introduces into its statements the very subjective element that true science professes to eliminate as completely as possible. Scientism assumes far more than the facts warrant. A case in point is the citation from Russell just mentioned. Any doubts Russell might have had about the end of things were purely academic. Facts, he maintained, led to the clear conclusions forced upon him through having no prejudice of a subjective character. Whether that was actually the case remains to be considered, but that his certainty is not shared by many other scientists is evident. To conclude from the facts that we are destined for extinction, for example, seems a leap of faith (atheistic faith) to some thinkers. Thus, Dr. Fosdick in *Dear Mr. Brown* tells of the radically different theories of two scientists — Millikan and Jeans — about the future of the physical universe. One of them thought it might be building up by inward re-creation, the other that it was blowing up by dispersing at a prodigious rate. At last Millikan wrote to Jeans saying: "The one thing upon which we can agree is that neither of us knows anything about it."[8]

We mentioned the success of science. But that view of science may be justified only if understood in a very limited sense. To appreciate its significance for the understanding of the universe as a whole and of the *ultimate* truth of things, one would have to define one's criterion of success. Success from one standpoint may be unqualified catastrophe from another. No one would dispute the fact that the guillotine is highly successful for the elimination of headaches, but disastrous to anyone who wants to keep his head. Science may produce the goods without thereby promoting the good. A fool can gain the world and lose his soul in the process (Mark 8:36). So, in giving young people the facts of life in a physical sense while withholding the vital facts of faith, we may be dispatching them on a dead-end journey with no return.

Take man's statement that he is a wonderful creature, as his scientific discoveries and clever inventions clearly reveal. Once more we are obliged to ask what his criterion of judgment is in making this statement. If man himself is the measure of all things, isn't he "assigning and marking his own papers" in declaring himself clever and wonderful? The fact of the matter is that man has been endowed with a brain and other powers which he neither made nor merited. With the talents given him he fashions sputniks to revolve around the planets. But these are faint copies of originals which were in existence for millions of years before man ever saw the light of day. When he lifts up his eyes to the one who created these (Isaiah 40:25-28), it's not surprising if he has second thoughts about his own cleverness.

INEVITABLE MYSTERY

What grounds exist for the popular belief that science is fast removing the mystery once attached to the world in man's eyes, providing him in the days of his "ignorance" with incentive to worship? The discoveries of science haven't done a thing to remove any of that mystery. Science "explains" one thing only by relating it to something else, which is equally mysterious. In a sense, the more the scientist discovers about something, the more mysterious it becomes. New horizons appear all the time the higher one climbs. More distant peaks, whose existence wasn't previously suspected, now come into view.

The real mystery seems to be in that creative source from which man derived, seeing that he had no say in his own being. The limits of his knowledge are defined by this unchangeable fact: of himself he knows neither his source nor his destiny. It isn't his advance in knowledge of the world around him, but his ignorance of himself that accounts for his condescension toward the belief that there is an ultimate mystery in life. If a little knowledge is a dangerous thing, a little more of it, as St. Paul says, "puffeth up" (1 Corinthians 8:1, KJV). Compared with what man doesn't know, and by himself never will, what he knows is the tiniest speck in infinite space. This givenness of the world and of the self is no hypothesis, but an eternal fact which any sound view of life is obliged to face.

The scientist who regards faith as a contradiction of observed facts ignores the fact that science, by its method of observation, concentrates on a *part* of reality. It sees only the outside of things. It is therefore debarred from that vast inner world of the human spirit, without which the knowledge of the world observed by the senses would neither be meaningful nor even recognized. Horace the computer was only repeating what "he" had been told. In principle his decisions had been made for him. And if he should slip up, no doubt he could be constructed to reveal a red glow, but the meaning of the blush would be hidden from Horace. Only the observer would know what it was supposed to be. Such knowledge wouldn't be gained by observation, but by inward awareness experienced by the observer himself. Should Horace default in any way, the guilt wouldn't be his, nor the responsibility. I suppose Horace could be fashioned to copy in his behavior a man who has a bad conscience, but a copy of a conscience is a contradiction in terms. What makes conscience in the moral sense is precisely that it is one's own, not something copied.

What is true of the sense of duty and responsibility is also true of the awareness of the holy and of the fact of worship. Only in the inner world of the spirit can these experiences be known. Doubtless a machine could be made to go through all the acts of worship, according to one meaning of "acts." But of the *fact* of worship it would know nothing. Assuming, as some do, that the computer can represent *all* reality and not just its exterior aspect, if the computer worshiped as a believer does, that would presumably establish that the invisible, eternal, and transcendent God was a reality! But quite evidently the motions of worship, whether the kind that can be observed in the outward bodily posture or only as electrical impulses within the brain, are external to the *spirit* of worship itself. I knew of a parrot who was adept at saying the Lord's prayer, but to imagine that he could therefore *pray* would reveal hopeless confusion between the sounds that are a vehicle of expression and the sense that employs the vehicle. The laws that govern the one are of a different nature from those that condition the other. If scientism's view of reality — that the space-time dimension is all — were true, it would, as G. D. Yarnold observes, "constitute an insurmountable barrier to any real understanding between the sciences and the Christian religion."[9]

But, as we have sought to show, the view that reality is in the last resort of only one dimension is a presupposition not found in the facts themselves, and one that doesn't make sense. It would mean that some day we could weigh ideas as you weigh pork chops, and dole out thoughts in centimeters. This presupposition accounts for the view mentioned earlier, that science, through its research in archaeology and biology, had exposed the fallacy of faith. But in reality, such a view was the result of scientism's illicitly equating outward description with inner explanation. But the terms *evolution, natural selection,* and *chance* were bandied about regardless. It was assumed that since purpose and a guiding hand couldn't be detected through a microscope, they couldn't be real. Such a conclusion was only possible for one who presupposed that the instruments and methods employed to investigate the outside of a phenomenon were adequate also to penetrate the inner mystery of the spirit. Purpose is evidently something which can only be grasped from within and consequently defies all attempts to photograph it.

DESCRIPTION AND INTERPRETATION

Another assumption of the scientist who confused interpretation with factual description is that uniformity in nature implies mechanical necessity. The relevance of that equation for our purpose is its effect on faith. For faith affirms that God, the Creator of the world, is also able to guide its movements as he wills. In other words, the closed-shop idea of nature must be jettisoned if faith is based on fact. Thus, Prof. Antony Flew writes on the subject in this manner: "The insistence of the scientist, in so far as he is simply a scientist, on always seeking strictly universal laws is itself rooted in the fundamental object of the whole scientific quest: if scientists are to find comprehensive explanations, they must discover universal laws. A scientist's refusal to accept the idea that in any single case nature has been overridden by supernatural events is grounded . . . partly on his commitment — which is chiefly what makes him a scientist — to continue always in search for completely universal laws, and for more comprehensive theories."[10]

The author of that statement virtually admits that the scientist is secretly walking by faith (though not in the Christian sense) and not by sight. For the scientist is "always in *search* for completely universal laws." So obviously he doesn't know that such laws exist. Further, Flew is condemning the scientist to eternal ignorance of what, apparently, is necessary for the prosecution of his work. For to establish *universal* laws is impossible without omniscience. Yet we are told that such laws are a dogma of science. Moreover, Flew is by implication admitting that what the scientist has hitherto succeeded in discovering about the way nature behaves cannot really depend on the fact of universal laws, for the scientist is still searching for these. Flew says: *"If* (italics mine) scientists are to find comprehensive explanations." But if not, what then? They have gotten on pretty well so far without them. What if only God can know comprehensive explanations? Must science then grind to a halt — on ideological grounds? Indeed, though the scientist may not take too kindly to his exclusion from omniscience, it may be all to the good from the standpoint of man's welfare.

That there is sufficient uniformity in nature for man to live on earth and develop in the personal sense to the highest degree needn't be questioned. It's the conclusion that therefore nature is a "no-go" area for the Almighty himself that makes faith prick up its ears. But uniformity of some kind and in a certain measure is clearly essential. Mechanical necessity is not.

Let us suppose a child goes to bed regularly every night when the clock strikes eight. A visitor from outer space who peers night after night through a slit in the curtains of the child's playroom might come to the conclusion that the behavior of the child in getting ready for bed was necessarily determined by the striking of the clock. But one night the other-worldly visitor witnesses a "miracle." The clock strikes eight times and yet the child goes on playing. Neither the clock nor the visitor knew that it was the child's birthday and that the rule had been relaxed for the occasion. So what had been interpreted as the action of rigid causality turned out to be the purposeful planning of personality. It is interesting to observe (though faith by no means depends on such an observation) that the concept of physical causality, as Yarnold remarks, has had to be abandoned by scientists themselves in respect to the sub-atomic world, so that exact prediction becomes impossible.[11]

Another popular fallacy, already mentioned, is that science is only interested in brute fact, that it deals with undiluted reality, whereas faith gets its own private wishes mixed up with everything. Hence, only science possesses the yardstick by which all that is real must be measured. But we have sought to show that to evaluate facts of the spirit in terms of space is to elevate absurdity above common sense.[12] You wouldn't, for instance, be able to detect integrity with the most penetrating X-ray machine. The so-called "truth machine" would be useless to anyone who didn't already know truth and lying as an inner awareness.

In any case, the scientist's observations, however keen, can take him no further than what his own limited mental constitution can grasp. "Immaculate perception," as Nietzsche calls it, is a myth. "It may be," writes Prof. Rhodes, "that the qualities that we measure have as little relation to the world itself as a telephone number has to its subscribers."[13] Actually, any judgment on the *ultimate* nature of the universe must itself be a judgment of value. So whatever the distinction between science and faith, it cannot possibly be that the former deals with hard facts and the latter with a hypothetical realm of values.

LIMITATIONS OF SCIENTIFIC EXPERIMENT

As for the claim that the experimental method of science gives it a great advantage over faith, one cannot but feel that this needs testing. It is made, we saw, on the grounds that science can go right up to its object, without having to take off its shoes and keep its distance, and that it can test its theories by what it sees to be fact. Yet we mustn't be too hasty in thinking that man will benefit by eliminating the sacred. If science were to wash its hands altogether of the sacred, we would have to look forward to a multiplication of Belsen, Dachau, Auschwitz, and Buchenwald. Unbridled scientism courts self-destruction.

If the human race were deprived overnight of all the spiritual furniture provided by faith, it would be in a bad way indeed. John Baillie is right in saying that if faith should languish, the scientific impulse would also eventually die. Having no worthy end, it would become just a dangerous tool. No doubt faith often falters in its interpretation of facts, but what it is after is vital for man as a human being. Hence Oman's observation — that science tells big lies in support of a little truth and religion tells little lies in support of a big truth.

According to biblical teaching, it isn't true to say that faith is barred from testing by experiment. To a decadent nation of old went the challenge: "Put me to the test, says the Lord of hosts, if I will not open the windows of heaven and pour down for you an overflowing blessing" (Malachi 3:10). And to a king in a crisis came the invitation: "Ask a sign of the Lord your God; let it be deep as Sheol or high as heaven" (Isaiah 7:11). So also to those who were weary of formal religion, and were seeking the reality that would renew the life of the spirit within them, was addressed the call: "If any one thirst, let him come to me and drink" (John 7:37). Thus it is not in the fact but in the method of testing that faith contrasts with science.

ASSUMPTIONS MISTAKEN FOR FACTS

We have sought to emphasize the distinction between the assumptions of certain scientists and the actual facts discovered by them. Before concluding, I propose to examine some observations of Bertrand Russell to illustrate this point. Now, in the words of Russell quoted already, we have what is clearly a manifesto, not of his factual findings, but of his atheistic faith. And that faith includes the following articles: (*a*) our end is ultimate oblivion; (*b*) science presents us with a world that is purposeless and void of meaning; (*c*) man was produced by blind causes; (*d*) man's loves and beliefs are the outcome of "accidental collocation of atoms."

First, we should note that if man's beliefs are just the outcome of a collocation of atoms, presumably *that* belief must take its place in the queue of accidents as well as any belief that contradicts it. So all beliefs cancel one another out and truth becomes a figment of the imagination. Yet Russell speaks of the "truths" he is seeking to propagate. "Only on the scaffolding of these truths," he says, "only on the firm foundation of unyielding despair" can we henceforth safely build. But, we are compelled to ask, what can "a firm foundation" possibly mean in a world ruled by accident? What can "accident" mean? Isn't it a purely relative term expressing our state of ignorance? If two cars collide when neither driver intended it, we call it an accident. But that only describes subjective intentions, not objective facts. From another standpoint, there is a perfectly good explanation for the "accident." And for that matter, if the world which now is (with all its beauty and purposive activity as seen in the life of man) is an accident, why must there be eventual extinction? Why shouldn't accident produce next time a realm of eternal bliss?

A second example of pronouncements that show how much easier it is to talk about facts than to face them is seen in a published report of a television interview given by Russell on a "Face to Face" program, which was doubtless seen by a great number of viewers. "When you are studying any matter or considering any philosophy," Russell said, "ask yourself only what the facts are and what is the truth the facts bear out. Never let yourself be diverted . . . by what you think would have beneficent social effects if it were believed, but look only and surely at the facts. That is the intellectual thing that I should like to say.

"Then the moral thing I should wish to say to them is very simple: love is wise, hatred is foolish. In this world, which is getting more and more closely interconnected, we have to learn to tolerate each other. . . . We can only live together in that way and if we are to live together and not die together, we must learn the kind of charity and the kind of tolerance which is absolutely vital to the continuation of human life on this planet."[14]

Despite the wisdom of much in that statement, many questions arise. First, granting that to ask after the facts is obligatory for everyone who wants to get at the truth, how does one get over the difficulty of finding them? When Russell declared that facts are an accidental collocation of atoms, was he reporting or theorizing? It's no use saying "turn to the facts" to settle the matter. The whole dispute is precisely about what the facts are. To a color-blind person the fragrance of a rose is a fact. Its redness is not. But to his friend, who has no sense of smell, the redness is a fact, and the scent is not. To Russell, God is not a fact. To St. Paul he is the only unconditional fact that exists. Who is telling the truth?

Second, Russell advises against letting the beneficent effects of a belief color our view of its truth or falsity. Yet his own view that love is wise and hatred is foolish seems to be based on the grounds that to believe otherwise must have disastrous consequences (we shall die together rather than live together). But on Russell's foundational principles we're doomed to eternal extinction, anyway. Whether we go *together* or not is a question of timing. And since there is no foundation but sand, isn't it somewhat foolish to expect any building, whether made of love or hatred, to stand at all?

Third, Russell regards the continuation of human life as the justification for ranking love higher than hatred. In that case, quality is servant to quantity. Faith, however, reverses this, declaring that the only valid justification for life's continuance must be the worthiness of its quality. "Whoever causes one of these little ones who believe in me to sin," said Christ, "it would be better for him to have a great millstone fastened round his neck and to be drowned in the depth of the sea" (Matthew 18:6).

Further, Russell would no doubt have been right when he said that the moral thing he wished to say — that love is wise and hatred is foolish — was simple, had he meant that *saying* it was simple. But the problem lies neither in saying it nor in getting people to agree with it. The problem is in acting upon it. It would be naïve to imagine that the heart of man was going to be moved by being told what was wise. Anyway, wisdom doesn't beget love. Only love can do that. The change in Saul of Tarsus was brought about "by faith in the Son of God, who loved me and gave himself for me" (Galatians 2:20). St. John writes: "He loved us, and sent his Son to be the propitiation for our sins . . . if God so loved us, we also ought to love one another" (1 John 4:10, 11, KJV). We don't love one another because it is wise to do so. Wisdom may have the dexterity to arrange the sticks, but only love can kindle the flame.

THE COOPERATION OF SCIENCE AND FAITH

The moral of all this is that we should neither lean too heavily on science nor castigate it, if we wish to face the facts. We have seen that life has deep dimensions outside the jurisdiction of science. "I am no more surprised," writes Sir Bernard Lovell, "or distressed at the limitation of the spectroscope in describing the radiance of a sunset or at a theory of counterpoint in describing the beauty of a fugue."[15]

Similarly, we must not leave it to science to create a "brave new world," which it was never fitted to do. Theodosius Dobzhansky, the world-famed biologist, writes about suggested programs for the genetic control of man, that "they presume that we know far more than we actually do about what kinds of genetic endowments would be best for man to have, not only at present, but also in the remote future. It can show no lack of respect for the greatness of men like Darwin, Galileo, and Beethoven, to name only a few, to say that a world with many millions of Darwins, Galileos, or Beethovens may not be the best possible world."[16] We may say, then, that were we to set out, with ever so much knowledge, to plan human life in the future, from its first stages to the minutest detail in all its later social relationships, we would still be confronted with the sobering challenge posed by Karl Mannheim: "Who plans the planners?"

That the faithful, like everyone else, benefit in many ways by the discoveries of science is too obvious to need elaboration. What isn't so commonly realized is the debt of science to faith. An instructive article appeared in the philosophical journal *Mind* nearly forty years ago on "The Christian Doctrine of Creation and the Rise of Modern Science," in which M. B. Foster showed how Christianity gave the green light to science for the pursuit of its method of observation and experiment. It did this by stressing God's revelation of himself as the God of order, who has made a world that can be fruitfully investigated by intelligence. It isn't, therefore, a world under the control of the whims of demonic powers. On the other hand, the world is not itself divine, and consequently may be investigated without outrage to its creator.

We have said that purpose is not discerned through a microscope, but that it is nevertheless a factor in the human set-up. We must go further and realize that man's purposing nature has the power to bless or to curse life, according to the spirit that rules his will. The techniques of science wait upon the man who employs them. The materials are the same for swords as for plowshares, for tanks as for tractors. The issue will be decided by the hand that works them. And this is where faith comes in.

CHAPTER FIVE

The Voice of History

The title of this chapter would have the same effect on many expert historians as the proverbial red cloth has on a bull. To talk about the voice of history, they would say, is simply to show one's ignorance. The "voices of history" might make more sense, perhaps, though to many history is just plain mute. So, according to this view, to ask whether history sustains or slays faith is to ask for trouble. Yet the Christian faith was proclaimed at the beginning by men whose message was inextricably bound up with historical facts. Our interest here is in the reason for this and in the question whether facts have come to light since those early days that would require history to "leave the witness stand."

THE AMBIGUOUS STATUS OF HISTORY

One reason for avoiding any appeal to history to commend the Christian faith is the uncertainty in many circles of the meaning of the term *history*. This may mystify those of us whose acquaintance with history is pretty much confined to the time when we took it in school. In those days we were expected to learn what happened to 1066. We read with lively interest about the number of wives Henry VIII possessed and dispossessed. At that time there didn't seem to be any problem about history — except the problem of remembering it. To say that "history is bunk" on the one hand and "history is a science" on the other didn't make sense. True, the former view was held by an industrialist and the latter by an historian. But Henry Ford and J. B Bury represent different factions found in theological, philosophical, and historical circles today. Between these two extremes are other varieties of historical interpretation relevant to the question of whether history gives any clue to the veracity of the Faith.

Before we proceed, it would be well to consider Bernard Lord Manning's warning to those who are tempted to make illicit capital, one way or another, out of history: "People who call for history to bear out what they say are likely to find history bearing them out indeed, but bearing them out as the young men bore out Ananias, and for a similar reason."[1] Manning deplores "the glibness with which men will trace what they are pleased to call the hand of God in history," because it "is enough to make unregenerate historians sneer and to shock those of us whose religion teaches that the ways of God are past finding out."[2]

THE IMPORTANCE OF HISTORY FOR FAITH

Having taken to heart that warning about a wrong use of history, we shall consider briefly why the early Christian witnesses laid so much stress on certain historical events in preaching the Faith to the world. One reason was surely the way in which they themselves came to know the truth of the gospel. They came to know it because of certain facts which had actually happened in this world of space and time. They declared that they were themselves witnesses of these facts. They had come face to face with a man who manifested in his own life, and created in theirs, a new dimension, promised long before, but never realized until then in human experience. How, exactly, they came to know that in Jesus of Nazareth God himself had assumed human nature, I sought to show in the opening chapter of this book. The point to be stressed here is the significance of their witness — that because they had encountered him as a fact of history, not because they had been inwardly moved by exalted ideas, they came to faith. And this point we must never forget: whatever theories men have spun through the centuries about the way we come to believe in God, the Christian faith was made known to the world by those who came to a knowledge of the truth of the gospel through its manifestation in historical fact. By no stretch of the imagination could they be called academicians or classed among the sophisticated thinkers of this world.

This fact has proved a stumblingblock to many "intellectuals." It seems almost as though they had been cheated somehow. To think that Tom, Dick, and Harry have actually found, through no genius of their own, what the professionals and experts were still fumbling for must hurt a good bit. Indeed, C. E. M. Joad came to a point when he didn't, at least implicitly, deny this. For he tells us that for many years he never bothered to give serious thought to Jesus Christ, he (that is, Christ, not Joad) wasn't intellectual enough. And this is how we give ourselves away, for it shows a bias that prevents us from coming to a knowledge of the truth, inasmuch as we may (even if unwittingly) be more interested in the process of finding truth than in the truth itself.

But the importance of history for Christianity isn't simply that it *happened* to be the medium through which the faith was made known to believers. We read that this *in vivo* method of communicating the way of salvation to man was chosen by God because of its momentous implications for faith. For one thing, it means good news for those who can appreciate facts when they see them, but who are incapable of following subtle and involved arguments. Jesus tells the congregation in the synagogue at Nazareth that his coming, as an historical event, to their midst was the fulfillment of the divine promise to bring "good news to the poor, to proclaim release for prisoners and recovery of sight for the blind; to let the broken victims go free" (Luke 4:18, NEB). This didn't mean that it was the illiterate who were poor and blind and broken, but it did mean that *everyone* was being reached by the gospel. It wasn't a man's intellectual qualifications that fitted him for the greatest of God's blessings to man. Christ explicitly stated that to "have a thing" about one's own capacity to penetrate the mystery of grace is to forfeit all knowledge of it. "I thank thee, Father, Lord of heaven and earth, that thou hast hidden these things from the wise and understanding and revealed them to babes . . . Come to me, all who labor and are heavy-laden . . ." (Matthew 11:25, 28).

We must not, however, run away with the notion that the gospel was for people who were a little simple. The plain fact is that this faith has, in the course of history, inspired the most talented specimens of the human race the world has ever produced. This holds true whether we are thinking of scientists, philosophers, artists, or experts in any other field of learning and culture.

What I am saying is that, to bring light to the whole world, God chose to give it in the only way all could see it. The eternal donned the garments of time. Truth became embodied fact. And the consequences of this are vital for faith. Not only does the incarnation of the divine enable all to see what otherwise must remain hidden, but second, it enables us to believe the incredible: right at the heart of the almighty power which created all things, at the heart of burning holiness, is the wonder of self-sacrificing love. What hadn't occurred to human thought became a matter of knowledge to the first witnesses of faith. Augustine tells us in his *Confessions* how startling was this witness to the presence of God among us. He had studied the books of the Platonists, who had no inhibitions about speculating over the divine. "But," he says, "that the Word was made flesh, and dwelt among us; this I read not there." And, of course, the assumption of flesh by the Son of God was only the first stage of the journey to Calvary of him "who, though he was in the form of God . . . being found in human form . . . became obedient unto death, even death on the cross" (Philippians 2:6, 8).

Third, the actual seeing of the divine glory in historical fact had revolutionary consequences not only for the way we *think* of God, but also for the response it claims in our whole attitude towards him. When the truth confronts us as a fact in the flesh, and not merely as a bloodless idea in the mind, it has a challenging power of its own. The believer knows that his faith implies a new way of living. St. Paul prefaced the passage we have just quoted from the letter to the Philippians with an exhortation about the kinds of everyday relationships which follow from the truth they had seen and believed. "Do nothing from selfishness or conceit, but in humility count others better than yourselves. . . . Have this mind among yourselves, which you have in Christ." The inescapable confronts us when fact is present. Theories and mere possibilities may be false and consequently have no authority over us.

Another consequence of the factual presence of the truth is the obligation, not only to try to live it, but also to spread it abroad. Here we are entering a field "strewn with the bones of controversy." To many it indicates the nadir of ignorance, not to say rock-bottom narrowness, to thrust our own faith down the throats of others who are just as good as ourselves. So it is reckoned incredible that in this day and age there can still be antediluvian types around who fancy that only they have the truth. Now, let it be made quite clear that narrowness, bigotry, and ignorance of a world "outside one's own little tub" have no affinity with genuine Christian faith. But it is equally true that authentic faith has no room, either, for the confused and emotive language that is frequently employed as a substitute for straight thinking. What passes for magnanimity may be disguised indifference. What appears as breadth may be nothing but superficiality.

To illustrate the point in question, whoever has a real concern for knowing the truth will seek the facts. Whether the facts discovered reflect well or otherwise on one's preconceived ideas is irrelevant. No scientist or physician who came across something he knew would make an untold contribution to the health of mankind could be exonerated if he put forward as hypothesis what he knew to be indisputable truth. No one would excuse him if he said he concealed the facts because he didn't wish to seem narrow, or because, had he come clean, it would have entailed upsetting deeply-held convictions of friends as capable as himself. Let us suppose, then, that he took the line that it would be wiser to work with his friends on a given patient by applying both his "cure" and theirs (which in fact negated his). What would we say? Shouldn't he have refrained from applying a "remedy" that he knew to be against the patient's interests, and bear whatever ostracism or criticism might ensue?

Or take another parable. Two men are fishing in a river within a short distance of each other. One is a surgeon and the other a butcher. Suddenly they see that someone has fallen in, hurt himself, and is drowning. Surgeon and butcher put down their rods, and with equal concern put everything they have into an attempt to rescue the drowning man. Thanks to the cooperation they display, they succeed. The surgeon sees that an operation is indicated, so he and the butcher proceed together to the door of the surgery. Then comes a little hitch, all because the surgeon has suddenly become uncooperative. The butcher has taken it for granted that he too would be taking a hand in the operating, so he is nonplussed at this turn of events. After all, he's no novice with the knife. Who does the surgeon think he is? He didn't despise the helping hand at the riverside; he was extremely glad for it. Why, then, the polite shaking of hands and "many thanks" at the door of the operating room? We don't need to ask that question to see the answer. Surely the interest of the patient is paramount now, and nothing else.

This parable, of course, doesn't give any excuse for superior airs on the part of the one who knows, or for a spirit of rudeness toward the one who is mistaken. The butcher may have been the better man, as man. Moreover, to bless, not curse, is the Christian witness's business, whether he is dealing with bitter and aggressive enemies of the Faith or with those who are only seeking to be loyal to whatever light they possess. (Only the ignorant deny the existence of light in non-Christian faiths.)

But the believer has to face other facts. For people in darkness to despise the light of candle isn't a good sign. But neither is it a good sign if people who know sunlight become content with the light of the candle. The commission of Christ was: "All authority in heaven and on earth has been given to me. Go therefore and make disciples of all nations" (Matthew 28:18, 19). To go with any other mission is to go alone, having forfeited the promise added: "Lo, I am with you always. . . ." And it is to go in a way that will turn the light that is in us into darkness. This will result not in the blessing of the nations, but in depriving them of what Christ came to give.

Nothing we have said claims to *prove* that what the early believers held to be fact must be so. Personally, I feel one has to be more credulous to deny that their witness was based on historical fact than to believe it. And there is no lack of scholars, past and present, who have scrutinized the facts with patent honesty and concluded that the Christian faith is based on hard historical truth. What we have tried to show is the vital part historical fact plays in the Christian message. To deny the one is to deny the other. To cite but a few of the many thinkers in this field: "Christianity's insistence on the uniqueness of the Incarnation and its preoccupation with history are inseparably bound up together; for history is essentially the sphere of the singular, the unique . . . the Christian belief in the Incarnation is not at all parallel to the oriental belief in avatars . . . and there is no parallel elsewhere" (H. H. Farmer).[3]

"The decision of faith . . . implies a new understanding of existence . . . Does not all this rest on the faith that a divine history has occurred . . . Does not faith therefore mean *aligning our existence with this series* of events hic et nunc?" (Oscar Cullmann).[4] Another rejects the view that "history must humbly confine itself to the lucid and meaningful description of ultimately meaningless facts"[5] (Langmead Casserley). And another stresses the paramount importance of undertaking a study of the "way in which relevation comes to birth and acquires some patterns of its own within the very process of history" as "one of the major ways in which we can make religious claims significant and relevant today." He points out that "it is especially indispensable to due appreciation of the claim to uniqueness in the Christian revelation" (H. D. Lewis).[6]

Others shy away from binding faith to history, for a variety of reasons. For example, it is objected that a faith based on so-called historical facts must share any uncertainty surrounding those facts themselves. In other words, if the foundation is shaky, isn't the whole edifice liable to wobble? But certainty in the abstract sense isn't available in any sphere which has to do with the facts by which men live. *Logically* all the New Testament witnesses could be either mistaken or born liars. But the man or woman who ponders their message deeply and listens to what they say seriously will find a fabricated Christ incredible.

DETACHING FAITH FROM HISTORY

Others have an idea that certainty about the facts would destroy faith, which calls for a "free decision" and therefore must not be compelled by knowledge. But this objection seems to confuse compulsion to recognize the historical facts and compulsion to respond with that faith we have called trust and commitment. If compulsion to acknowledge the historical facts themselves inhibited faith, then the early believers who tell us they witnessed the facts would be prevented from exercising faith! Our argument in this chapter is not that fact forces faith, but that faith cannot be divorced from fact. So, if writers like Van Buren and others were saying only that knowledge of public facts about Jesus does not *itself* produce faith, they would be in line with the actual teaching of the Scriptures. Even the enemies of Christ, as we have seen, had to admit the fact that he cast out "devils," but instead of believing in him, they interpreted his actions by saying that he was possessed of the "prince of demons" (Mark 3:22).

Another objection to believing that the ultimate truth of God came in Christ is that it is incredible that universal truth and the Savior of the world should have become known to us only through the experience of a group of nonentities who happened to live in little Palestine. But even if we cannot understand why God should have chosen this way, we are certainly confronted with the mysterious effects of his so doing. The light which shone from the shores of Galilee and the hill of Calvary nearly two thousand years ago scattered more darkness in three centuries than the culture of Greece and the might of Rome could have done in thirty. Hence the observation that the pagan hordes who conquered the Roman legions, when they descended upon the "Eternal City" in the fifth century A.D., were themselves conquered by the gospel of the Nazarene. What began insignificantly, became in the end the means of changing the world like the grain of mustard which "grows up and . . . puts forth large branches, so that the birds of the air can make nests in its shade" (Mark 4:32). History does not lack examples of the "weak" things of the world confounding the mighty. So events must be assessed on what they accomplish, not by a prejudiced theory which asks: "Can any good thing come out of Nazareth?" The only answer is: "Come and see" (John 1:46, KJV). After all, a beautiful child may be born in the slums, and a lily may grow up from a dump heap.

FAITH'S RELATION TO HISTORY

Supposing, now, we grant that no reasonable doubt attaches to the substantial historicity of the records that tell us about the Jesus who once went about doing good, who possessed exceptional ability to do "mighty works," who died upon a cross and afterward appeared alive to his disciples. How do these facts create faith? How do we know their *significance?* In other words, what warrants the translation of powerful deeds into miracles, a death *because* of a sinful world into a death *for* such a world, a rising of one who had been dead into the resurrection of the Son of God? How do we move from the good man, Jesus, to the God-Man, Christ? What justifies this leap? Aren't we leaving facts behind? It seems that we can only answer by saying that what appears from the outside as a leap, from within the world of faith is experienced as an illumination. It is neither a movement of logic, on the one hand, nor a case of wishful thinking on the other. The facts are essential for faith, but don't create it. "We *beheld* his glory," says John, not "We deducted it," nor "We had a strong feeling." It is the logic of the whole situation, not the logic of a syllogism, that enables us to see a miracle in the mighty work. The deeds themselves led men to ask, "Who is this?" For the answer, those deeds had to be seen in the context of the words and the life of the one who performed them. It was not to leave men open-mouthed, but to open their eyes, that Christ came to the world.

The mighty works, then, were intended to conduct, not to compel, men to faith. They were signs for those who wanted to know the way, the truth, and the life. (A "good" historian may be ignorant of the good news.) Yet the challenge that "any faith must let itself be exposed to the observable facts of the world in which we live"[7] is one the Christian faith has never sought to evade. The first witnesses proclaimed the good news on the very spot where the facts could be checked. They were specifically commanded to begin in Jerusalem before bearing the message to the ends of the earth. "We are given enough light," says Pascal, "for those to see who only desire to see, and enough obscurity for those who have a contrary disposition." It is often taken for granted that only believers are guilty of polluting the purity of objective fact with subjective prejudice, so it is well to be reminded that unbelief can be born from a "contrary *disposition.*"

To treat historical events as though they were physical objects is to assume that man has as little to do with the making of history as he has with the constitution of the object he examines in the laboratory. If this were true, man would be doomed to stare at the passing world around him as sheep or cows do, with the result that he would be bound to miss seeing any meaning that history may have been purposed to teach him. His failure to see would be due to the fact, as Pascal puts it, that he was not disposed to be illumined. Had Solomon treated events as one treats things, he would have missed the truth about the rightful owner of the tug-of-war baby, whom he proposed to cut in two and divide between the disputants. His knowledge of human nature, and how it differs from physical nature, enabled him to interpret the real mother's reaction to his proposal. He knew that truly objective examination of events involving persons required subjective participation on the part of the one who wished to get at the true meaning of the facts.

History is perhaps a science, as Bury said. But, when he went on, in an attempt at being objective, to say that it was "no less and no more," he was forfeiting the means of discovering the actual truth. To imagine that the arena of history is in principle only a big laboratory is to suffer from "a sick retina." As Carl Michalson puts it, "Studies in abnormal psychology have shown that the spiritually-anxious lack the capacity to interpret facts but will compile them industriously, a phenomenon which has led Merleau-Ponty to observe that 'the sick like the learned' verify their hypotheses by assembling facts."[8] As Professor Coulson observes, "He who stops at the facts misses the glory."[9]

The point, then, is this: facts which are open to public observation only become meaningful in any profound sense where there is illumination that is not a public experience. But this isn't to say that such illumination is only another name for subjective fancy, which has no relation to truth. To experience the illumination one must be in a certain frame of mind. Hence the words of Christ quoted by St. John: "Whoever has the will to do the will of God shall know whether my teaching comes from him or is merely my own" (John 7:17, NEB).

Doubtless, interpretations may be purely subjective, and probably often are — but this weakness is no monopoly of believers. The historian who declared that the drama of history was not written by God, but by generals and dictators, wasn't any less subjective than men of faith. Why pick on generals and dictators? They are largely the end-products of multitudinous factors too labyrinthine to trace. It may be just as true to say that the drama of history is written by politicians or bishops. And if it's true that the hand that rocks the cradle rules the world, even what historians write may have been decided no less by godly (or ungodly) parents than was the course of history determined by the length of Cleopatra's celebrated nose, as Pascal says.

THE MESSAGE OF THE RESURRECTION

In no instance does the interpretation of an historical event need more sensitive handling than the resurrection of Christ. The skeptic takes it for granted that his resurrection was meant to be proof of life after death, and this suggests that it is the product of the wishful thinking of the timid and the bereaved. But this view of the Resurrection ignores some vital and relevant facts by making what is just one element in a situation dominate the whole. It's true that the Christian regards the Resurrection as a sure foundation for the hope of survival after death. Christ has transformed the tomb into a tunnel. But were that the entire significance of the Resurrection, it would considerably strengthen the hand of the skeptic who dismisses it as a fantasy based on hearsay — something which simply doesn't happen in history, but which belongs to what David Hume calls "those superstitious delusions" that "will continue as long as the world endures."

The resurrection of Christ was regarded by the early witnesses "as of first importance" (1 Corinthians 15:3) not simply because it assured the believer of an extension of life in the beyond, but because of its power to create a new dimension of life here and now. St. Paul said that without the Resurrection he had nothing to preach and his hearers had nothing to believe. Martha of Bethany, like most of her compatriots, already believed that her brother would "rise again in the resurrection at the last day." What she had yet to learn was that the resurrection in its profounder sense was present *now* — in the person of Jesus Christ. For it is he who reclaims man from "the second death" and restores to him the divine heritage he had forfeited. This he accomplished by a death which is crucial for the forgiveness of sins. "If Christ has not been raised," the apostle wrote, ". . . you are still in your sins." The implication here is that the primary purpose of the resurrection of Christ was to light up the Cross, not the grave. It illumined Calvary, not just as the place where an innocent victim was slaughtered by ungodly men consumed with pride, jealousy, deceit, and prejudice, but as an offering of a divine sacrifice on behalf of such men.

Therefore the sacrifice of Christ is unique. Through it God brings into being a new creation. The Resurrection reveals this uniqueness. In view of this, the objection that history does not supply us with other instances of dead men rising from their graves loses its force: history had never before witnessed a Christ. In the incarnation the Lord of history was invading history.

No advance in historical studies since the time when the Faith was first proclaimed can pretend to have hit upon new facts that would discredit the claims of the early witnesses. Nor is the argument that recent research in biology shows the irreversibility of the process by which human cells deteriorate after death any more to the point. The argument itself is based on an unscientific assumption: that the laws of biology are independent of a Creator — or, if not that, that the Creator would have no good reason ever to reverse them.

But we have already seen that St. Paul tells us both that a good reason exists for reversing those "laws" and what that reason is. It is to illumine history as the arena of divine activity for the redemption of the world and for the creation thereby of a new humanity. The Resurrection shows that history is not simply the display of "one emergency following upon another as wave follows wave . . . the play of the contingent and unforeseen," as H. A. L. Fisher saw it. But whereas Fisher tells us that "the intellectual excitement of discerning in history a predetermined pattern has been denied"[10] to him, the New Testament witnesses, with equal openness, assure us that they had no choice about seeing the pattern. "This Jesus God raised up, and of that we are all witnesses" (Acts 2:32). They proclaimed that message without hesitation in the very place where those whom they were addressing had only a few weeks before crucified the Christ. They tell their judges in Jerusalem: "We cannot but speak of what we have seen and heard." St. Paul, likewise, is careful to point out that both he and his fellow-believers were not reading the Resurrection *into* history, but declaring it as a revelation through history: a revelation which, though predetermined, was totally unexpected.

Those first witnesses didn't arrive at the belief that Christ had risen by reflection upon the extraordinary spiritual strength and joy they had suddenly experienced. They didn't go out to Jerusalem and tell the populace: "It appeared to Cephas, then to the twelve . . . that Christ must surely be alive; for otherwise how can one account for the way we feel?" Rather, St. Paul wrote: *"He* appeared to Cephas, then to the twelve . . . he appeared to more than five hundred brethren at one time . . . he appeared to James . . . he appeared also to me" (1 Corinthians 15:5-8). It was the Resurrection, in fact, that gave them a gospel to preach.

That they had witnessed the appearances, and not simply imagined them, was evidenced by the power of Christ expressing itself through the amazing works of healing they performed in the presence of the public (Acts 4:16). But the greatest witness of all to the fact that Christ had risen was the power of the message to produce new men: men who reflected in the way they lived something of the glory of the risen Christ himself. They had been "raised together with," says one who had once been a violent opponent of the gospel. The message, then, is about a unique power that had broken into history, and which could never have evolved out of it. The message not only divides believer from unbeliever, but also the Christian faith from every other religion. For as H. D. Lewis puts it, other religions "have nothing of the . . . finality of the Christian claim . . . no once for all redeeming event whose significance is to be preserved at all cost."[11]

The Christian proclamation was not born, then, of the disappointed hopes of a little coterie that had been reduced to a state of neurotic make-believe. On the contrary, the Faith was preached and practiced by men of character, sanity, freedom, and honesty — men who couldn't be contained within the precincts of temple walls or in private gatherings of the pious. They burned with passion for the one who had salvaged them from a life of slavery to self and restored them to a life of liberty in the service of God. And genuine passion for Christ meant a genuine concern for those for whom Christ died.

It is understandable, then, why the risen Christ should have appeared only to a chosen few rather than to the public indiscriminately or to anyone who happened to be around. For the Resurrection was not something to be bandied about for sensation purposes. It wasn't intended to be a scoop for the journalist, but a message through those who had been possessed by its sacred power. Hence, the all-important factor was the quality of the witnesses; three men of integrity carry more weight in the work of the Kingdom than three hundred crooks. The message of the Cross and the Resurrection, then, was intended to effect a change of heart in the serious, not to produce a state of euphoria in the credulous.

To the power of this change of heart, history bears abundant witness. "The birds of the air have lodged in the shade of that tree on which were nailed the sins of the world." As B. L.

Manning remarks: "Our literature, our language, our philosophy, our art, our social ideals . . . have Galilean elements. The earth of Christendom is crammed with the kingdom of heaven, and every common bush is afire with the power of the Son of God."[12] So the penetrating power of the gospel makes us aware of a reality that calls us to faith. The ring of the authentic is recognized in the manner that faith not only faces facts but transforms them.

CHAPTER SIX

Appeal to Experience

It was graduation day. The Cambridge don thought it was a fitting moment, just before the capping ceremony, to deliver a little parting homily. "You realize, of course," he said, "that this isn't the end of your education. In fact, it's only the beginning. *We* have simply given you the tools; only experience can teach you how to use them."

Most people would doubtless concur with that. Experience, you might say, is the university of the masses. It is regarded as both the most expensive and the most authoritative seat of learning. Experience usually stands for direct contact with something, as opposed to acceptance of what someone else says about it or mere speculation on the matter. Not infrequently we were told as omniscient adolescents: "I can't argue with you, but experience proves otherwise." Our key witness concerning the facts of the world around us — the world of sense-perception — is experience. The most ingenious argument has to take off its hat when experience appears on the scene. Yet it's significant that when experience starts making pronouncements on matters of faith, one soon feels a change of climate in philosophical circles today; religious experience is now well used to being given the cold shoulder, which suggests that it's a waste of time to give it a hearing at all.

Within the camp of believers, however, many swear by experience in spiritual matters. It is their irrefutable answer to those who aren't all that impressed with the witness for faith given by reason, science, and history. Who, then, has the truth in this matter? Is religious experience an imaginary ivory tower to which the routed flee and feel safe? Or is it a refuge and strength which can stand up to the severest testing of the toughest facts? In brief, does "religious experience" give good grounds for faith, or not? I shall attempt here only a helicopter view of the territory we have entered, and leave the layman who is prepared to trudge through jungle and wade through swamp to consult the readily available guides on the many problems that confront the explorer in depth in this particular field. Here, however, we must be content to glimpse the landscape as a whole.

RELIGIOUS EXPERIENCE

Let us first try to be clear on the meaning of "religious experience." Although this experience may assume different forms, the point at which it is of interest to faith is where it claims to have *knowledge* of God, and not simply strong convictions about him. The experience may involve intense feelings: feelings that arise from contemplation of the thought of God or from reflection on his handiwork. The experience may take the form of a seeming transportation to a different dimension from what is normal: a dimension where time doesn't exist and where consciousness of oneself has vanished. Few men and women, comparatively speaking, seem to have enjoyed such a mystical experience. Those who have known it claim to have been in direct touch with the abiding reality which lies behind all else and from which everything, in the last resort, proceeds. On the other hand, religious experience may refer to a quiet but highly significant illumination of the mind and warming of the heart, which has been shared by countless believers throughout the ages and which transforms the common stuff of life, investing it with a profound purpose in which God's hand is discerned as a living fact.

OBJECTIONS TO RELIGIOUS EXPERIENCE

The claim made by religious experience has frequently brought together some strange bedfellows. In fact, it seems that once more Pilate and Herod become friends on this issue. For not only skeptics, but a number of believers as well, look with considerable suspicion on this "experience" argument. Some believers fear that it *threatens the authority of reason,* for it substitutes for a firm, rational foundation one that is notoriously vacillating and unreliable. Other believers see in experience a *challenge to the primacy of revelation,* by making man the source of our knowledge of God, instead of God's own infallible disclosure of himself. Yet others are only concerned in this matter with *the futility of employing the argument as proof to unbelievers* of God's existence. They don't wish to question its genuineness as evidence to the one possessing the experience, but they see the importance of recognizing its limits, just as St. Paul regarded the experience of speaking with strange tongues as of no edification to the outsider (1 Corinthians 14:23).

Before we consider what the skeptic has to say in this context, let us look briefly at the remarks of those who fear for the rightful place of reason and of revelation through an illegitimate elevation of religious experience. We have already observed in the foregoing chapters that in *some* sense of the word, reason must never be jettisoned in matters of faith, unless chaos is to take over. The object of faith is a God of order, not of confusion (1 Corinthians 14:33). Were reason completely abandoned, it would invite all kinds of extravagant and contradictory claims, with the inevitable consequences of devaluing rather than promoting faith. But we have also seen that what often passes for reason may in fact be simply an amalgam of "logic" and prejudice. A religious experience that shatters one's former way of life, such as was encountered by Saul of Tarsus on the road to Damascus, is relegated to the category of the psychopathic, despite its liberating and integrating power. It must always be borne in mind, then, that although reason may serve to detect what is not authentic, it doesn't itself possess the capacity to discover truth.

As for safeguarding the element of revelation, this also may not be played down without disastrous consequences for faith. There is, however, a false division implied in the question, "Which comes first: revelation or experience?" For there could be no awareness of a revelation that wasn't experienced. What Christian faith cannot allow is that a genuine Christian experience is possible without revelation. If *every* belief is interpretation, no gospel exists. Views, however exalted, cannot be equated with news. And news must come *to* us; it cannot arise from us. "Faith comes by hearing" (Romans 10:17, KJV). Nor is the Christian faith claiming any special concession when it stresses the need of something that is not simply one's own subjective interpretation if man is to have knowledge at all. Even *sense*-experience is only possible if something is presented *to* us which is not *of* us. It is certain that man can only come to a knowledge of God if God chooses to make himself known. And this is what God has chosen to do, according to the Faith. In the words of St. John: "No one has ever seen God; but God's only Son . . . he has made him known" (John 1:18, NEB).

When we look at *what the skeptic thinks* of religious experience, we note here again a mixture of truth and error. The skeptic does indeed concede that the believer is certainly having some kind of experience, which accounts for the blissful feelings and strong convictions he reports. No doubt, he may say, the castle of experience is cozy enough, and its occupants are clearly having the time of their lives. But the trouble about that castle is that it has no chinks through which outsiders may peep and see for themselves what exactly is going on inside. So those who are interested in facts can hardly be expected to be impressed with what the privileged occupants say. Since no feeling can speak, it is unable to say *of what* it is a feeling; hence the need for interpretation. And this immediately exposes the believer to the arena where faith will have to fight for its claims; in fact, for its life. For many theories claim to explain religious experience without bringing God into the matter at all. Thus, if prayer raises you to the third heaven, doesn't cannabis transport you there also? And if the rods of the magicians of Egypt could be turned into serpents like the rod of Moses, Pharaoh can't be blamed, surely, if he concludes that there is nothing really to choose between "the Lord" and magic.

Sometimes the skeptic turns the religious argument against

the believer's case. He argues that if someone who claims to have had direct experience of God (as one who is perfectly good) holds that his experience is proof that such a God exists, then by the same logic someone who claims to have direct experience of a god (who is all-evil) may regard *his* experience also as proof of the existence of such a being. Madden and Hare in *Evil and the Concept of God* write: "We have a friend who reported having a mystical experience with an all-powerful, all-evil God — 'It was ghastly,' he said, shaking at the recollection of it."[2] At other times, the boomerang method of refuting the believer will assume a less sinister form. Prof. John Hick (who is himself a confirmed theist) represents the argument as follows: "If it is reasonable for one man, on the basis of his distinctively religious experience, to affirm the reality of God, it must also be reasonable for another man, in the absence of such experience, not to affirm the reality of God."[3]

As we have said, the skeptic is doubtless right in some of his observations. Mere feeling does not inform us of its cause. The mere claim to know God obviously doesn't prove that the claim is justified. But is religious experience mere feeling? The skeptic *assumes* it is. And this is tempting for two reasons. In the first place, he doesn't know the experience himself; and second, it may well be the case that only the feeling can be described in words. Thus we can say, "I was filled with a wonderful kind of joy," or "I was in the grip of terror," or "I felt deeply humbled." However, it doesn't follow that the feelings make us say we had an experience of God. The way we use the religious experience argument often gives this impression, and the skeptic has every right to reject it when this happens.

But what if it was the unique awareness of God that produced the feelings, rather than vice versa? That is the way the Bible presents the matter. When God addresses a man, it says, the call to response contains the assurance that it is God who speaks. To question the authentic thing is also to be aware that there is treachery in the inward parts — that the conscience is not clear, that there is a twist inside. We secretly know that the evidence is sufficient and that to require further proof is to prevaricate. We are not here talking about logic, but about facts of experience.

The skeptic who rules out the possibility of such direct intuition of God, which is not simply a subjective interpretation, does so because he assumes that his own interpretation of what the world is like is true. But according to the skeptic's reasoning, even if there *were* an almighty God who wished to make himself known to man, without involving man in any doubt at all about it, he would be forbidden to do so! Now, we aren't denying that Ayer is right in saying that "a mere appeal to intuition is worthless as a test of a proposition's validity,"[4] if the test in question is meant to establish validity to one who has no such intuition himself. But the same argument holds good in spheres other than that of religious experience. Take, for example, the process of logical reasoning: the fact that a given argument is seen by a clear thinker to be logically sound is no proof of its validity to one who cannot see it for himself. Now, the Bible does not claim that revelation was intended to prove validity in the logical sense, but rather to illumine reality and truth in a concrete situation. That is why the early witnesses to the gospel preached the object of faith — Jesus Christ — not its logic, when they called men to believe.

EXAMINATION OF THE OBJECTIONS

But what about the other objections to the religious experience argument? It would seem that the flaw they all contain lies in their failure to distinguish between the outer form of an experience and its inner meaning. Thus a superficial resemblance between the effects of cannabis and the effects of prayer should not be taken to imply that the cause is identical in both cases. Superficially, the house built on sand may *appear* to rest on the same kind of material as the house founded on the rock. The truth of the matter, however, is already known to anyone who has done any digging. The effects of the elements will eventually make it known to everybody else (Matthew 7: 24-27). The New Testament contains many warnings against misleading appearances that would "lead astray, if possible, even the elect" (Matthew 24:24). It emphasizes the necessity of testing the spirits "whether they are of God" (1 John 4:1). The first epistle of John applies such tests — not to prove that there is a God, but to show the infinite gap that can actually exist between experiences that on the surface appear identical.

The statement, "I have had an experience of an all-powerful, all-evil God," is grammatically identical with the statement, "I have had an experience of an all-powerful, all-good God." Does that imply that the one claim is as good as the other? That can evidently be the case only if we have nothing at all to go on except rival claims. But when the *content* of the two statements is considered, there is more to it than just that one is as good as the other. For the self-destructive character of the one experience, were it followed through with all seriousness, would surely reveal that the person who had been in touch with what he called an "evil God" was insane. Everything that makes for edification and integration in life, everything that enables "the fruit of the Spirit" to appear, would become impossible. Of course, if the skeptic wishes to argue that insanity is as good a guide to truth as "the reality principle," he can do so, but only at the cost of throwing reason, in its wider sense, to the winds.

As for the third objection to the argument from religious experience, it is no doubt true to say that if the only ground for affirming the existence of God is one's possession of religious experience, then no one without such an experience may affirm God's existence. But some seem to have confused this conclusion with one that is totally different, and one which doesn't at all follow from the argument in question. For they appear to think that absence of religious experience is a ground for not believing in, or even for denying the existence of God. This is to regard the statement, "I have had an experience of God," as being *logically* parallel with the statement, "I have had no experience of God." But there is a clear fallacy in treating a negative statement as we treat an affirmative one — in a logical sense. Thus, to see a rabbit in a field would (normally) prove that there was a rabbit there; whereas *not* to see a rabbit there would indicate no more than that the person who couldn't see one just couldn't, and nothing more. The reasons for that could be many: his eyesight might not be too good, or he might have been looking in the wrong direction, or the rabbit might have popped into a thick clump of grass.

I should stress once more that I have *not* sought to show that the religious experience which many claim to have had proves the existence of God to those who have had no such experience. I am saying that this is no reason to write off religious experience as useless for proof, even to those who have had the experience. Subjective that experience may be; but isn't experience of the sense-world also in the first place subjective? And how can *that* experience mean anything to those who are incapable of having it themselves? So it appears that the taboo on religious experience talk among so many contemporary philosophers isn't basically due to the fact that it is subjective, but to the fact that it contravenes the dogma that the rightful monopoly of the route to facts belongs to a syndicate of the five senses. But this dogma itself is either based on experience or on subjective interpretation; in which case (on the skeptic's own logic) it is useless as proof to anyone who doesn't already believe it.

EXPERIENCE AND WISHFUL THINKING

It is probably true that much that passes for experience is not authentic. It is no small temptation to project one's own wishes on to the cosmic screen and then call the whole process "experience." Now, "in a philosopher," as Professor H. H. Price puts it, "wishful thinking is a plain breach of professional duty."[5] What isn't so clearly recognized, as I see it, is that wishful thinking is no less a transgression for the man of genuine faith. Price goes on to say that the philosopher who believes in God is peculiarly vulnerable to the charge of wishful thinking, since the state of affairs he believes in would be the very best one conceivable if it actually existed. To this we would reply: It all depends. It depends, for one thing, on one's attitude to the truth. God isn't Santa Claus. I am quite sure that Professor Price doesn't himself mean this, but many writers today take it for granted that the Father in heaven is in fact only a glorified Father Christmas. They don't seem to have heard the words of Scripture: "Note then the kindness *and the severity* of God" (Romans 11:22). Moreover, the Christian heaven, to those who will hear nothing of repentance and faith, is the nearest thing to hell they can imagine. Only the other day in the course of a television discussion, when a member of the panel innocently volunteered some consolation by saying that we shall *all* be included in the end (that is, in glory), a well-known rationalist reacted with the rebuff: "But I don't *want* to be included." As Terence Penelhum observes: "The human being's constant thirst for rationality . . . is not always beneficent in its results. It can lead to our creating beliefs to match our attitudes . . . and to our destroying beliefs when our attitudes change (which is what happens when faith is lost and belief abandoned)."[6]

EXPERIENCE AND REVELATION

The skeptic's charge of wishful thinking against the believer who claims to have religious experience, then, is a weapon which can hurt the skeptic himself just as much. It's clear that to deny the possibility of any knowledge of God may be no less a product of wishful thinking. What is equally clear is that if religious experience, based on God's revelation of himself, does not yield *knowledge* of God (as opposed to material for human interpretation only), then the Christian faith is definitely not "with it." Some other forms of faith may still survive, but not faith in the distinctively Christian sense. Christian faith is a response to the grace which has first come to us, not to a hypothesis of our own construction. Otherwise, the believer would be like a man who makes a vow of fidelity to the woman he wishes to marry, subject to the condition that she is not simply a hypothesis. I don't mean to imply that our knowledge of God is in every respect parallel to our knowledge of fellow mortals, but it is pure assumption to conclude, therefore, that God can't be known at all. It is not reporting of fact.

The claim to have had a revelation of God which gives knowledge isn't however, a claim to omniscience. The believer, like everyone else, may misinterpret many of his experiences and at times mistake for a revelation what turns out to be his own interpretation. He may even have "visions" of what isn't there at all. To revert to our rabbit illustration: it isn't impossible, of course, to "see" a rabbit in the field when actually no rabbit is there. But the mistake could only be recognized when contrasted with a genuine experience of seeing a real rabbit. As I look through the window in my room, I see in a neighboring field what I take to be a farmer and a black lamb. But on closer examination I discover my mistake: the farmer turns out to be a scarecrow and the lamb a poodle. Now the fact that my first interpretation was mistaken doesn't mean that *all* interpretations may be equally false, or, indeed that there may not even be any rabbits and farmers. For in that case, I couldn't possibly know that any of the interpretations were false, since the detection of a mistake depends upon knowledge of the imitation.

The revelation which is the primary datum in Christian religious experience, although it doesn't dispense with reflection or guarantee that everything believed to be revelation is so, can't itself be the fruit purely of reflection. Revelation is illumination which neither the objective facts nor human reflection provide. Many homes in Wales have a well-known picture called "Salem." It portrays a scene in a country church where an elderly woman is making her way to a pew, while other worshipers bow their heads in prayer. It is commonly believed that the woman's shawl displays an image of the devil's face. His profile, with forehead, nose, and eye, was included in the pattern (so it is said) to convey some moral about the devil in church. When I first saw "Salem," I couldn't make out the profile of the devil at all. But when it was traced for me with a finger, I could see the point: in fact, the difficulty afterward was to miss it. But was it really meant to portray the devil? Or was the image simply a coincidence produced by the pattern and folds in the shawl? The only way to settle this question is to hear what the artist himself has to say. Short of that, the matter must be left to speculation, despite the availability of relevant "objective" facts.

Similarly, Christian faith remains a guess unless God has spoken. But what makes that faith what it is, is precisely that

God *has* spoken. Indeed, he is essentially the God who speaks. An inferred God or a probable God or a remote one (like Aristotle's, for example) could never bring man to faith. For the believer, to talk about a God who doesn't speak is like the remark someone made of Wagner's music: that it's really better than it sounds! What kind of music could that possibly be?

In light of the fact that the Christian knows God solely on the grounds that he has spoken, many attacks on the Faith are seen to be beside the point. They assume that only if scrutiny of objective facts can prove God's existence is it possible to know him at all. An article by Sir Alfred Ayer in the national daily newspaper of Wales[7] illustrates this. Under the title, "Do you believe in God?" is printed the headline, "Such scant evidence of his existence." Now, apart from the fact that Prof. Ayer in this article is denying the existence of something which in *Language, Truth and Logic* didn't even have a meaning (and, consequently, as Ayer admits, can neither be affirmed nor denied), we observe that the God in whom Ayer is interested is one who, of necessity, can only be reached from man's side. However, the God of the Christian faith is essentially one who speaks to man. That is why he is known at all. True, if he weren't there he wouldn't be able to speak. But we may not take it for granted that we can only know whether he is there or not if we can find him along the route we ourselves have laid down. Listening may succeed where searching has failed.

The God who has never spoken would be the "absentee landlord" whom the tenants have never seen and whose demise would be simply the death of a hypothesis. But even if we could establish a God who created the world and yet be strangers to his voice, we would be devoid of knowledge as far as the living God of faith is concerned. On the other hand, once man hears God speak, the whole created order is transformed. The starry heavens above and the moral law within, which have made so deep an impression on multitudes beside Immanuel Kant, are now seen in the light of the Creator's "eternal power and Godhead." Facts already familiar take on a new significance, being invested with a glory to which we were hitherto blind.

THE SIGNIFICANCE OF THE MORAL LAW

Such also is the case in respect to the fact of obligation and the fact of guilt. Atheists and unbelievers alike recognize these as facts of experience. All know the sense of "ought," but not all recognize its profound significance. For the atheist it is "just one of those things." It "happens to be there" as a mysterious power that can create feelings of guilt if resisted. On the other hand, to the believer it speaks of the nature of God and of what is required of man. That men can recognize the moral law without seeing in that law a proof of God's existence doesn't imply that there could be such a law without God. Had the Prodigal Son become afflicted with amnesia in the far country, he would perhaps have forgotten the existence of his father, but he would still have been living on his father's money. Indeed, should the Prodigal's memory be restored to him, he would be the first to recognize this fact.

We can appreciate that the significance one sees in the moral law has practical consequences of a vital character when we consider further some remarks made by Ayer in the article mentioned. He maintains that the fallacy of proving God's existence from human morality "depends upon the assumption that only purely selfish behavior is natural to man." In other words, that man has to be *told* to be unselfish and threatened with law. But, adds Ayer, "the only criterion for deciding what is natural to man is what men actually do. . . . If experience shows that they act unselfishly as well as selfishly, we can only conclude that both types of behavior are natural." Now, apart from the fact that such an argument is itself based on an assumption — namely, that man has no obligation to any power higher than himself — it implies that man cannot do any perverted acts. For since the natural is what men actually do, "perverted" forms of behavior are not in fact perverted at all. They are as natural as any others, seeing that men actually practice them.

But the believer sees mirrored in the moral law something of the majesty of the one who is the source of the created order, including his own being. The duty to do what is right and the obligation to pursue the good is neither a dumb mystery nor simply the product of human policy for making life in society viable. Were the moral law mere policy, guilt would not be possible as we know it in its power to put us to shame. We would only know the so-called "false guilt" — which terrifies, but does not convict. For the power of true guilt is not a force that frightens by threats. Rather, it searches and exposes a breach of faith within, making a man aware of its source as transcendent to him and yet one in which he lives and moves and has his being. It is this awareness that enables man to stand for principle in the face of overwhelming numerical opposition, indicating that truth and right and goodness, in the moral sense, have nothing to do with majority vote. Similarly, it is the intuition of the holiness of God, from whom man has derived his being, that accounts for the sense of the sacred in human relationships and in the significance of personality.

PRAYER AS A MEETING WITH GOD

Further, the believer has access to the source of all power in a way that cannot enter the experience of one who denies the reality of God. I have in mind the way of prayer. For the act of prayer is the meeting place between man and his Maker. In prayer God does not merely speak to man, but communes with him. This is indeed the profoundest level of human experience. Man does not then think of God in utilitarian terms (a God whom he can use), nor in hypothetical terms (a God who is inferred from something other than himself). Rather, he is known as a presence who illumines and transforms his whole being. Only this meeting place makes it possible for faith to become knowledge. Only through the experience of prayer can man know that God answers petitions, which, to a mere spectator, might be regarded as coincidence. And in prayer the worshiper experiences the otherness and the nearness of God together; to pray is to draw near to the "throne of grace," where God, although enthroned in his otherness, is seen to be a gracious God in his nearness.

In order that man may seek God in such a manner, the divine hand may lead him along various paths. The promptings of the Spirit may be felt in the experience of bitter disappointment, of frustration and restlessness, of guilt that weighs us down, or of the success that humbles. But he who responds in faith to such promptings soon discovers that the meeting place with God is not a creation of wishful thinking. He enters into an experience beyond anything he had imagined, just as the Queen of Sheba, when she saw with her own eyes the glory of Solomon and his court, remarked: "Behold, the half was not told me." So also in the divine presence: the believer becomes aware of what had not entered the heart of man. It is like discovering that eating not only removes the pain of hunger but also imparts strength. Likewise, the deeper the soul enters into the life of prayer, the stronger it becomes and the clearer is its vision. We can then appreciate why Dante discovered, to his surprise, that faith yields far more than comfort. It lifts us up in a way that enables us to face problems instead of fleeing them.

In the experience into which prayer alone can lead us, not in the abstract arguments of logic, the believer comes to *know* what to the spectator cannot be other than a theory or an opinion. I don't mean that the believer's knowledge, which is imparted to him at the throne of grace, consists of intellectual explanations of all his problems. It isn't incumbent on God to answer all the questions that puzzle us. Some problems are a means of challenging the depth of our trust in God. We are the richer because of them since we are led to closer fellowship with God himself. And this more than compensates for the absence of an intellectual solution, since it produces a tranquility which no "proof" can bestow, even in storms that threaten our existence. Thus, to the question addressed to Jesus by the terrified disciples in a violent tempest, "Teacher, do you not care if we perish?" his answer was, "Why are you afraid? Have you no faith?" (Mark 4:38, 40).

FAITH AND SUFFERING

It isn't my intention here to discuss the "problem of evil," which some writers claim is sufficient to invalidate faith once and for all. Let it suffice to observe that authentic faith has never shirked the matter of evil. On the contrary, it was to face evil that Christ came in the first place. The believer cannot agree with what is today commonly taken for granted — that even if evil doesn't clearly disprove the existence of God, it does "count against" belief in him. In fact, it can only count against God if we arrive at belief in him by counting. And that is not the way that God has seen fit to make himself known, as I have sought to show. It is in terms of power, rather than of propositions, that faith receives the answers. After all, one thing is more serious than the *problem* of evil, and that is *evil* itself. It is worthy of reflection that one can be far more concerned with the problem than with the evil. But it is on the evil that the gospel concentrates. Hence: "The reason the Son of God appeared was to destroy the works of the devil" (1 John 3:8). And he did this, not by conducting seminars, but by sharing our sorrows and bearing our sins. It was by his power — the power of his presence — that the martyrs in the arena could bear the unbearable. Nero might photograph from the grandstand their incredible courage, but only those actually facing the suffering in the service of their Lord knew the secret of their strength. It will be recalled how Christian in Bunyan's *Pilgrim's Progress,* when taken into the house of the Interpreter, marveled that the fire could continue to blaze away despite the fact that water was being poured upon it. Only when Christian was taken to the other side of the wall did the answer become clear. For there was "a man with a vessel of oil in his hand, of which he did also continually cast (but secretly) into the fire."[8]

We can understand, therefore, why the Apostle Paul could say: "The gospel I proclaimed did not sway you with subtle arguments; it carried conviction by spiritual power, so that your faith might be built not upon human wisdom but upon the power of God" (1 Corinthians 2:4, 5, NEB). Paul knew that power firsthand. In the vicarious suffering of Christ, the reconciling love of God had become a fact revealed to him by the presence of the risen Lord. Hence his exhortation: "Let us even exult in our sufferings, . . . because God's love has flooded our inmost heart" (Romans 5:3-5, NEB). Possessed by this transforming experience, he *knew* "that there is nothing in . . . all creation that can separate us from the love of God in Christ

Jesus our Lord" (Romans 8:38, 39, NEB). He had proved for himself something of the power of the Son of God, who had made of nature a sacrament, of blood a healing stream, and of death itself a gate to eternal life.

CHAPTER SEVEN

The Glory of Faith

Glory and faith, for the believers, were inseparable. You can't read the New Testament without feeling that a "stuffy" Christian is a contradiction in terms. The witness of men of different temperaments and cultural backgrounds throbs with the joy of freedom and fulfillment which faith in Christ brought into the lives of those who had believed the gospel. Paul exulted in what he called "the light of the glorious gospel of Christ" (2 Corinthians 4:4, KJV) and referred to Christ as "the Lord of glory" (1 Corinthians 2:8). John wrote, "We have beheld his glory," adding, "from his fullness have we all received" (John 1:14, 16). Peter spoke of the "joy unspeakable and full of glory" which is the possession of those who had come to faith (1 Peter 1:8, KJV).

What has been cited confirms the word of Christ, as reported in the Gospels, about the effect of faith on the believer. For example, he depicts the "kingdom of heaven" as "treasure in a field, which a man found . . . then in his joy he goes and sells all that he has and buys that field" (Matthew 13:44). And in his intercessory prayer for his own, Jesus addressed the Father thus: "I speak these words so that they may have my joy within them in full measure" (John 17:13, NEB).

THE SOURCE OF THE GLORY

Words like *joy* and *glory* need to be spelled out in the

down-to-earth climate of thought that characterizes our age. Otherwise they may well be taken to denote emotional experiences which, like the foam on the surface of the stream, are at the mercy of every passing breeze, rather than the strong undercurrent which determines the direction of the flow until the ocean itself is reached. It is well, therefore, to realize at the outset that the glory, joy, peace, and fulfillment of which the early believers spoke were invariably anchored in the fact of Christ: in his sacrifice on the Cross, in his resurrection from the dead, and in his ascension to the Father. The blessings of faith are bestowed by Christ on the believer. They are not worked-up feelings, nor are they dependent on vacillating circumstances. "Peace I leave with you: *my* peace I give to you; not as the world gives do I give to you" (John 14:27). We have already seen that it is *his* joy Christ gives to the believer. Similarly, "The glory *which thou has given me* I have given to them" (John 17:22). What this implies in practical terms is that faith has access to an unfathomable and unfailing source of power and glory which, *when appropriated,* works a revolutionary change in the life of the believer.

THE NATURE OF THE GLORY

The glory of that change we may describe as constituting both a new beginning and a new ending. The one is a new creation and the other a new destination. In other words, the glory of faith comes into its own as it manifests itself in that love and hope which St. Paul coupled with faith in the famous thirteenth chapter of the first epistle to the Corinthians. This new creation of love and the new destination of hope I shall now seek to consider briefly before drawing the present discussion to a close.

The glory of the new creation lies both in its depth and in its breadth. It is deep because it implies nothing less than a new nature. It is broad because its consequences reach far beyond the inner private life of the believer out into the world of human relationships and conditions surrounding him.

Something of the depth of the glory may be appreciated as we ponder a few of the terms employed by the New Testament writers to set forth the consequences of faith in Christ. In saying that the believer is a new creation, I was borrowing a phrase of St. Paul's. He once told the believers in Corinth that "if any one is in Christ, he is a new creature" (2 Corinthians 5:17). This new creation is a new nature. "Put on the new nature (KJV — "new man"), created after the likeness of God" (Ephesians 4:24), which in turn, is explained as the result of a new birth. "You have been born anew, not of perishable seed but of imperishable; through the living and abiding word of God" (1 Peter 1:23). And, "unless one is born anew, he cannot see the kingdom of God" (John 3:3).

Now on the face of it, and outside faith, statements like that may well sound as nonsensical today as they did at first to the pious Jewish council member, Nicodemus, when he visited Christ at night in the hope of discovering the secret of the Rabbi from Nazareth. But the context of all these verses should make it clear, even to an observer who is not a believer, that they have a profound, concrete, and practical significance. For the "new creation," the "new man," and the "new birth" refer not to the elimination of self-identity, but to the possession of what I call a new center of gravity.

The new man in Christ is not simply the man who adopts as his ideal Christ's standards of living, but the man who knows something in the depths of his being of the pull of the living Christ's presence and power. And it isn't the presence of an alien, but of one to whom the believer belongs and from whom he does not wish to be set free. In a manner of speaking, it is the presence of another self whose will is to become also one's own. Hence the apostle's declaration: "It is no longer I who live, but Christ lives in me; and the life I now live in the flesh I live by faith in the Son of God, who loved me and gave himself for me" (Galatians 2:20).

THE FREEDOM OF FAITH

The result of being thus possessed is freedom. But it is freedom in depth, because it is freedom from the dominion of the ego. To say it is freedom from fear is ambiguous and can be quite false. For a kind of salutary fear is as necessary for the soul's development as the fear of fire is for one's biological existence. Hence the word of Christ: "Do not fear those who kill the body but cannot kill the soul; rather fear him who can destroy both body and soul in hell" (Matthew 10:28). There is a false freedom which results in moral obtuseness and spiritual blindness. It is the "freedom" that gives free rein to desire and indulges the "instincts," on the grounds that they are natural, in a manner contrary to the purpose of nature. It is the freedom of the alcoholic's access to liquor and of the child's to a razor. It is the freedom that fancies it can slay guilt by burying it, not knowing that guilt thrives underground, where it finds the most productive soil of all for its deadly work. On the other hand, faith knows that guilt can only die as it is brought to the surface, faced, and forgiven. The gospel knows no other freedom which is authentic (John 8:36) and which merits the appellation "the glorious liberty of the children of God" (Romans 8:21).

True freedom, then, is a condition within. It is freedom from oneself. Hence the advice given to a rich lady by her psychiatrist — not to add a fourth to her three existing country retreats, because she would meet herself when she got there. The freedom of faith, on the other hand, isn't found in human nature, but is possible only as we become "partakers of the divine nature" (2 Peter 1:4), that is, of God's Spirit. For "where the Spirit of the Lord is, there is freedom" (2 Corinthians 3:17). Paradoxically, therefore, only the man who is possessed of another can be in possession of himself. But the paradox is resolved when we realize that the nature of that other is pure, uncompromising, and unconditional love. Where love is supreme, freedom is impregnable. A slave who was given his release could, according to Mosaic law, declare, "I love my master . . . I will not go free" (Exodus 21:5, NEB), and would thereafter remain his master's servant for the rest of his days. The believer likewise finds his liberty in being bound by the cords of love to him who alone can bring him fulfillment. Paul was jubilant in calling himself "slave of Jesus."

In Jesus Christ the fullness of the divine nature is made manifest: the fullness of "grace and truth." The glory of the gospel is that it makes known the God who is *both* grace and truth. Were he only grace, he would have nothing to give. Were he only truth, he would not have given anything.

The glory of the new creation is also revealed in its breadth, not only in its depth. In other words, the glory of the new man reveals itself not by introspection but by action. This is how Paul puts it: "For the love of Christ controls us. . . . And he died for all, that those who live might live no longer for themselves but for him who for their sake died and was raised" (2 Corinthians 5:14, 15). The believer knows he is self-centered, and no worldly education or technical skill can make him anything else apart from divine grace. But he also knows that real love does not live for itself. Because such love is the very nature of God (1 John 4:8), "whoever would save his life will lose it" (Mark 8:35). Love, if hoarded, will die; only in giving can it grow.

HOW FAITH IS RELATED TO LOVE

The earthen vessels of human nature, in which believers have this treasure of God's love, never do justice to the glory of its transcendent power. We may, as one theologian observed, measure the depth of the well, but not the height of the sky reflected in it. Even so, if the love of Christ is not in any measure in the believer's life, if the fruits of the Spirit never appear, grace, according to New Testament teaching throughout, has not begun its work in that life at all. For the love of which the gospel speaks, in uniting man with God, by that very act begins its work of uniting men with one another. The logic of living faith is clear: "If God so loved us, we also ought to love one another" (1 John 4:11). A receiving of grace that doesn't entail becoming gracious is a caricature of faith, not its creation. Jesus said, "He who believes in me . . . *out of* [not simply 'into'] his heart shall flow rivers of living water." John, the writer, adds, "Now this he said about the Spirit, which those who believed in him were to receive" (John 7:38, 39).

The observation that "truth without practical love is a lie" echoes what lies at the center of New Testament teaching about the connection between faith and works, between our relationship to God and our relationship to our fellowman. In short, grace is indivisible. And this means (among much else) that distinctions between black and white, educated and illiterate, rich and poor, are transcended in the life of faith. For the separation of love for God from concern for one's fellow-men is a creation of feigned piety. "If any one says 'I love God,' and hates his brother, he is a liar" (1 John 4:20). That is strong language, but it is reiterated in one form or another time and again in the New Testament. "Faith by itself, if it has no works, is dead" (James 2:17). "If I speak in the tongues of men and of angels, but have not love, I am a noisy gong or a clanging cymbal . . . and if I have all faith, so as to remove mountains, but have not love, I am nothing" (1 Corinthians 13:1, 2).

The glory of faith, then, is not simply in what awaits the believer in the future, but in what has already taken place in his life here and now. There is no humbug about faith; it cannot serve God in the church and fleece others in business. Loving God and cold-shouldering one's neighbor are incompatible. God accepts no gift from us where there is meanness toward others, or where the spirit of reconciliation is absent (Matthew 5:23, 24; Mark 7:11-13).

In the face of these facts, we can appreciate St. Paul's exclamation, "Who is sufficient for these things?" And we can see why even he didn't claim to have yet arrived at the perfection of love, mighty man of faith though he was. The more he contemplated the unfathomable mystery of grace, the greater was his wonder, and the more evident it became that it was the full-time calling of a dedicated life "to comprehend . . . what is the breadth and length and depth, and to know the love of Christ which surpasses knowledge" (Ephesians 3:18).

In the love of Christ alone are the infinite dimensions of divine grace to be seen. What often passes as love is simply a deceptive veneer — which accounts for the facile manner in which the word *love* trips over the tongue today. But the Scriptures bid us beware of imitations; they fail the crucial tests both of life and death. In the shop windows of Connemara, the visitor will sometimes come across two broken stones set side by side. They have been broken to reveal the difference between the genuine Connemara product which retains its distinctive beauty at any given point, and imitation stones made elsewhere and sold in Ireland to unsuspecting customers. The foundation of the believer's faith is also one in whom no dross of self could be detected, "our living Stone" (as Peter called him) "— choice and precious in the sight of God" (1 Peter 2:4, NEB). In the final test, when broken on the cross, he moved a tough Roman centurion, who was standing opposite him and saw how he died, to exclaim, "Truly this man was the Son of God" (Mark 15:39, NEB, footnote). He led St. Paul to write later to other Romans the triumphal words "I am not ashamed of the gospel: it is the power of God for salvation to every one who has faith" (Romans 1:16). The apostle is not referring here to the power that blows the whistle, but to the power that drives the wheels. "For our gospel came to you not only in word, but also in power . . . you turned . . . to serve a living and true God" (1 Thessalonians 1:5, 9). Such service was the fruit of the Spirit, not of human willpower. It was service by which human relationships in the home, society, industry, and all walks of life were transformed. Not only John Wesley, but every true believer, is to see the whole world as his parish. The sweep of Christian love is as broad as mankind.

FAITH AND HOPE

Another aspect of the glory of faith, mentioned earlier, was a new destination — which is the object of the believer's hope. As love looks both upward and outward, so hope looks forward. And just as Christian love is incomparably more glorious than any love human nature of itself possesses, so the believer's hope far transcends in glory the substitutes commonly offered for it today in both secular and religious circles.

To talk of hope, in the New Testament sense, is very suspect in the present philosophical and theological mood — which indicates how infectious is the skepticism that regards as imaginary anything that does not fit into the purely earthly dimensions of the sense world. It appears that looking forward to what lies beyond this life signified a flight from the most obvious fact of all: the finality of death. Philosophical analysts have even sought to prove that the very notion of a man witnessing his own funeral is *logical* absurdity. This popular fashion of settling issues of great moment, such as the question of personal immortality, is, as H. D. Lewis rightly remarks, "deceptively simple."

But the more subtle attack on Christian hope comes today from those who purport to interpret the Christian message to the contemporary world. The climax of the glory of that message, it is said, is the self-sacrificial act of love manifested in the Cross. One is given the impression that to stress the resurrection of Christ is not only irrelevant, but almost irreverent. ("Isn't anything after Calvary an anticlimax?" as it were.) We are, in effect, exhorted to keep our feet firm on this earth, to withstand the temptation to look to any "beyond" for our comfort, if we are to make the Christian faith credible to man come of age.

The plausibility of the interpretation in question is not difficult to appreciate when we consider, on the one hand, the widespread character of modern skepticism and, on the other hand, the way in which it cashes in on what we may call half-truths. Thus, it is true that nothing is *nobler* than the Cross. On Calvary we see the highest stooping with amazing love to rescue the lowest. It is also true that some seem to regard the Resurrection as a kind of emotional eraser, a means of counteracting the painful memories of the sacrifice, a way of drying the eyes of those who have to flee facts because they can't "take it."

At this point we seem once more to find man putting asunder what God has joined. For the glory of the good news, as proclaimed in the New Testament, consists not only of the noblest sacrifice, but also of a victorious and invincible one. Were it not for the fact that Christ had manifested himself as risen, the noblest might well have been the saddest. In other words no such thing as Christian hope would exist. The "good news" would be bad news, and "*Good* Friday" would be the biggest misnomer of all. It is all very well for us today to think that faith in the noblest should be enough to win our loyalty, without the help of props. But quite another matter is whether we would be able to believe this were it not for the fact that the early believers proclaimed the Cross to be a triumph. And it is certain that *they* could only know this because of the fact of the Resurrection.

The New Testament never presents the Resurrection as an event that eclipses the Cross. Nor is the Resurrection regarded as a compensation for the sacrifice. It is, rather the consummation of it: the destination of Calvary, not a by-pass of it. We read that on the evening of the Resurrection day two disciples were coming away from Jerusalem "talking with each other about all these things that had happened . . . looking sad" (Luke 24:14, 17). From the evidence at hand they had every reason for being sad, but not because their admiration for their late leader had diminished. (We read that they acclaimed him to the "stranger" who joined them as "a prophet mighty in deed and word before God and all the people" — v. 19). They were sad and dejected because their admiration was now devoid of hope: it couldn't create faith. "But we had hoped," they added, "that he was the one to redeem" (v. 21).

Then something happened that kindled in their hearts an unquenchable fire. It changed the direction of their journey and sent them back again to Jerusalem with a transformed spirit: the spirit of hope and glory. The transformation had begun when the "stranger," the risen, but as yet unrecognized Christ, opened their eyes to the real facts of the situation. "Was it not necessary that the Christ should suffer these things and enter into his glory?" (v. 26). So the glory of faith isn't only that it is faith in the suffering, for Christ said "and *enter into* his glory" *after* the cross.

But the glory isn't just in the Resurrection either. Rather, it is in a cross that was destined for resurrection, and in a resurrection that is only possible through the cross. Hence the apostle's consuming passion: "that I may know him and the power of his resurrection, and may share his sufferings, becoming like him in his death, that if possible I may attain the resurrection of the dead" (Philippians 3:10, 11). A Christianity, therefore, which can preach self-sacrifice without the victory that conquers suffering, or one which glories in a victory that doesn't demand suffering, is a faith from which the glory has departed.

Hope, then, is a major factor in the Christian faith; for the new creation is set in a new direction, having a new destination. Authentic faith speaks in this manner: "The sufferings of this present time are not worth comparing with the glory that is to be revealed to us . . . because creation itself will be set free from its bondage to decay and obtain the glorious liberty of the children of God . . . For in this hope we were saved" (Romans 8:18, 21, 24). Another witness tells how "the God of all grace, who has called you to his eternal glory in Christ" (1 Peter 5:10), has begotten us "anew to a living hope . . . to an inheritance which is imperishable, undefiled and unfading" (1 Peter 1:3-4).

Thus the gospel reverses the "law" of material nature, as it reverses the "law" of human nature. For as nature invariably empties our lives and fills our graves, Christ fills our lives and empties our graves. But the glory lies not simply in the empty grave but in the fullness of the new life that emerges from it. To live again without being "born again" would only be perpetuating the *length* of existence, which could be anything but heaven. The filling of life with divine love gives depth to Christian hope and rescues it from length without depth, from quantity bereft of quality. What the New Testament calls "eternal life" doesn't refer merely to unending existence; it refers to a new quality of life. That quality is such that time, even endless time, cannot erode it; it is the life of God himself and is therefore endless as well as full. It is unfailing as well as unfathomable.

To try to counteract an "other-worldly" faith by substituting for it a purely worldly one is disastrous. That would be like seeking to teach a lesson to a pendulum that was swinging too far in one direction by pulling it as far as possible in the other direction, thereby providing it with momentum that would send it flying again to the other extreme. Similarly, a faith that belittles Christian hope will beget spiritual sterility, just as a false other-worldly faith does.

Faith, in this present existence, travels through tension-territory; it both sees and does not see: "As it is, *we do not yet see* everything in subjection to him. *But we see* Jesus . . . crowned with glory and honor" (Hebrews 2:8, 9). "The good fight of faith" is a fight. It isn't a journey in a cozy limousine, but neither is it in an impossible jungle with uncertainty whether a way out exists. The life of faith, though not easy, isn't a matter of hit or miss, either. To change the metaphor, the storms may shake the ship, but they can never sink it. As one witness puts it, "That hope we hold. It is like an anchor for our lives, an anchor safe and sure. It enters in through the veil where Jesus has entered on our behalf as forerunner" (Hebrews 6:19, 20, NEB).

THE HOPE OF PERSONAL IMMORTALITY

Our hope is the hope of *personal* immortality. It isn't the spurious hope which simply believes in the perpetual continuance of the human race rather than of any individuals who comprise the race. If each generation ends as the individual does, all hope is annihilated at the gates of death. A thousand million zeros don't add up to more than one zero.

In any case, the faith that the human race will persist has no basis in merely natural facts. It is the product of wishful thinking unless we have something other than the evidence of nature to go on. For if the race hasn't existed *from* eternity, why should it exist *to* eternity? "People like to feel," writes Dorothy Emmet, "they live in a 'friendly universe' that makes sense; and a record of their theologies is largely . . . a record of the intellectual houses they have built in order to come in out of the rain."[1] Whatever impels people in general to build their intellectual houses, the New Testament men of faith maintain that the believer's hope is not the creation of what he likes to feel about the universe, but is constrained by confrontation with facts: the fact of God's power as manifested in the Resurrection and the fact of his love as revealed in the Cross. For it doesn't make sense that the God who brought to man redemption at such a cost should commit the redeemed again to eternal oblivion. Since "love will never come to an end" (1 Corinthians 13:8, NEB), we see why the Good Shepherd gave his life for the sheep in order "to give them eternal life" so that "they shall never perish and that no one might snatch them out of his hand" (John 10:28).

THE POWER OF HOPE

Again, Christian hope isn't the slogan, "Don't worry, it may never happen." Rather, the believers found it a dynamic power given to face whatever happened. It challenged both life and death to separate it from the love of Christ (Romans 8:39). It's a power that illumines, purifies, and inspires. It illumines by throwing light on the real meaning of life. Seen in their eternal setting, values assume a different color. The things we worry about most are seen, in the light of eternity, to be the trivial things they are. The things we regard as of no consequence for our everyday living are now recognized as the things that count. Eternal perspective changes the color of things just as artificial light in a shop deceives us about the color of some cloth until we see it in broad daylight. The believer's hope makes it impossible for him to regard man as a blind accident of nature, a chip of wood swept along by the flood, the mere victim of circumstances. Nor can the man of faith see life simply as an opportunity for self-indulgence while the going is good. On the contrary, life becomes a means of growing up into the fullness of the divine love as made manifest in Christ, not, "Let us eat and drink, for tomorrow we die" (1 Corinthians 15:32).

This illumination is therefore a medium of purification. It cleanses the soul by purifying it at the center. It judges our self-centeredness, which is the root of all that defiles, in the light of the self-abandonment revealed in the Redeemer. So, "everyone who has this hope before him purifies himself, as Christ is pure" (1 John 3:3, NEB). Our hope isn't hope for compensation for being "good," a payment for burdensome service on earth. It is, rather, hope of a consummation of what has already been initiated by grace. It is service in greater fullness and in eternal freedom. In the language of the New Testament, to be "*in* Christ" (2 Corinthians 5:17) creates the hope of being "*with* him" (Colossians 3:4), which in turn leads eventually to becoming "*like* him" (1 John 3:2). Nothing less than this is "the hope of glory."

But the effect of this hope isn't only good lives, but the receipt of joy (the "fruit of the Spirit") that possesses therapeutic power. What shook the world about those first believers wasn't just their patience and determination in their times of trouble, but also the way they could sing in the thick of it. "Let hope keep you joyful" (Romans 12:12, NEB) was the exhortation of one who was able to say, "With all our affliction, I am overjoyed" (2 Corinthians 7:4).

Those believers could rejoice when castigated and dishonored for the name of Christ (Acts 5:41). This joy is the mark of that fulfillment which Christ promised to the believer. It enabled them to sing praise to God when fastened to the stocks in the prison cell (Acts 16:25-30). And as the Ethiopian eunuch began the life of his newly-found faith rejoicing, so the great battle-scarred Christian warrior Paul looked forward to finishing it in the same spirit (Acts 20:24). It was the same joy that, according to Henry Venn's physician, kept that Anglican saint for another fortnight as he looked forward to entering the glory beyond.[2]

THE HOPE OF HIS COMING

The New Testament writers tell us that Christian hope is not only inspired by where we are going, but also by the one who is coming. The promise of Christ wasn't simply that he would prepare a place for his own, but that he would come again for them (John 14:3). He did, indeed, come again *in* them, when the promised Spirit took possession of them at Pentecost. But they declared that he would, according to his promise, return in power and that the pattern of this world would fold up. They saw no hope in a world, confident of its power to save itself, which rejected the Savior sent by God.

We have even less ground for placing our hope in man today. Just as the brains of Greece and the might of Rome miserably failed to bring true freedom to man in the days before Christ came, so the multiplication of amenities, and education in the "know-how" of things has left man without hope. He still inhabits a dark and collapsing world. Death is still the dissolution of achievement and the burial of hope.

But those "who have set their hearts on his coming appearance" (2 Timothy 4:8, NEB) are bidden, amid "the distress of nations . . ." and untold terrors, to "look up and raise your heads" (Luke 21:28). This isn't to have one's head in the clouds while refusing to face the facts on earth. It is an exhortation to draw inspiration for "the work of faith and the labor of love" (1 Thessalonians 1:3) from the steadfast hope sustained by the promise and power of God.

For the believer, therefore, facing the fact of life and the fact of death is a matter of faith from start to finish: faith in the one unchangeable fact — he who is "the same yesterday and today and forever" (Hebrews 13:8).

CHAPTER EIGHT

The Birth of Faith

The Christian message from the very beginning had one purpose: to bring men to faith — a faith that would be a living fact in the lives of the believers. The original witnesses to the gospel didn't regard themselves simply as purveyors of interesting theories about the relation of God to man. They didn't go around with speculative ideas or with thought-provoking subjects of discussion which men might argue about at will. They weren't even concerned simply to introduce to the world a high code of ethics, a system of Christian principles, that would provide a sound foundation for an integrated and decent society.

The facts about the Faith were proclaimed with such earnestness and dedication so that faith might become a fact for those who heard the message. Something had happened from God's side in order that something might happen in all whom the good news had reached. And that something, as we have seen, was nothing less revolutionary and momentous than a new birth. As H. D. Lewis observes in discussing belief (but in another context): "It is not enough to be on the way; we must arrive."[1]

FAITH AS A LIVING RELATIONSHIP WITH GOD

St. Paul tells the Christian converts in Ephesus that his prayer for them was that Christ might dwell in their hearts by faith (Ephesians 3:17). This implied that the message he brought to them was meant to go deeper into their lives than the intellectual and aesthetic level, deeper even than the moral level. At these levels nothing that happens to man need result in that radical change which is the inevitable consequence of living faith. If the message doesn't reach the heart, man will still regard himself as the master of his fate and the captain of his soul. The "old man" will be in charge, even after deciding to adopt new principles for his guidance. And if Marx could say against Hegel that we must change the world, not merely interpret it,[2] how much more may it be said of Christ that he came not just to reason with man but to ransom him.

To admit Christ into one's life in a consultative capacity is to miss the whole point of the gospel. To admire Holman Hunt's *Light of the World,* which portrays Christ with lantern in hand knocking on a door, is one thing. It is another to open the door from within to the living Christ, to say, "It is no longer I who live, but Christ who lives in me." A portrait of a person, be it ever so striking a likeness to the living thing, is still more striking in its unlikeness. It is something about which you may speak but which you cannot address nor hear speaking to you. It is significant that the greatest expositor of the Faith was also its greatest missionary. Paul the scholar and thinker was completely at the service of Paul the ambassador, who in turn was proud to call himself a bondservant of Christ.

RESISTANCE TO FAITH

This personal factor in faith constitutes the major stumbling-block in the gospel and accounts for the resistance it evokes. For faith, in confessing that Jesus Christ is Lord, renounces the right of self-determination. It hands over the ego's seals of office. That is why I said that faith implies a radical and revolutionary change in the life of the believer.

The radical implications of faith explain the bitter opposition it can arouse, opposition found both in secular and religious circles. Paul and his companion were accused of "turning the world upside down" (Acts 17:6). Demetrius, the silversmith, organized an infernal mêlée in the city of Ephesus when he saw the revolutionary consequences of faith in Christ. He warned his fellow-craftsmen that if this gospel is allowed free rein, "This trade of ours may come into disrepute" (Acts 19:27).

Nor has the passage of years softened the resistance to faith. Thus, Renford Bambrough, in a chapter entitled "Praising with Faint Damns," tells how he agreed to serve on a committee of a Heretics Club in Cambridge, a club apparently dedicated to discuss philosophical, religious, and other questions in an "uncommitted" spirit. But he soon found that every member would have to subscribe to a Rationalist Press Association magazine and that he himself was about to be unseated for his unorthodox opinions — "to be expelled from the Heretics for heresy." Bambrough adds that another met a similar fate at the hands of the Cambridge Humanists Society, when Dr. Hanson, an agnostic, incurred the wrath of the members by his cogent reasoning against the oversimplification of which his humanist colleagues were guilty. Apparently, he was lambasted for "playing into the hands of the enemy, the 'black beetles' in clerical collars."[3]

Opposition may sometimes be concealed under intellectual expression. Bertrand Russell was once asked what he would say if after death he found himself confronted by God. He replied: "I shall say to him, 'God, why did you make the evidence of your existence so insufficient?' "[4] The assumption here obviously is that the evidence for the truth, not our desire for it, is at fault. In other words, God is to blame, if anyone.

The New Testament makes it clear that, if we face the facts honestly, our real problem isn't the truth we don't know, but what we do with the truth we do know. As Gilson observes: "There is an ethical problem at the root of our philosophical difficulties, for men are most anxious to find truth, but very reluctant to accept it. . . . Finding out truth is not so hard; what is hard is not to run away from truth once we have found it."[5]

THE BIRTH FROM ABOVE

There is, then, such a thing as insisting that truth may only come to us along the predestined grooves of our prejudices. It is we who have the right, so we suppose, to make the demands, not the truth. On a visit once to Copenhagen, I recalled how I had read of a visitor who stood before the famous statue of Christ in the Cathedral there, and that the guide had told him that to see the real beauty of the statue it was necessary to kneel down. Apparently, the work had been so executed that only at a particular angle would it be properly appreciated. So it is with truth. Neutrality, where ultimate truth is concerned, is a myth, for that truth makes demands such as nothing else makes. Hence the sobering word of Christ: "He who is not with me is against me, and he who does not gather with me scatters" (Matthew 12:30).

Resistance to the faith that demands new center of gravity is also found in religious circles. Gresham Machen recounts how he heard a preacher pray in a village church. "After quoting the verse in Jeremiah which reads, 'The heart is deceitful above all things, and desperately wicked,' he said, in effect . . . : 'O Lord, thou knowest that we cannot accept this interpretation; for we believe that man does not will to do evil but fails only from lack of knowledge.' "[6] Machen goes on to commend the preacher's frankness and to condemn his paganism. That preacher represents quite a numerous and popular company of religious men and women today who cannot see that the heart of man is as wicked as all that. They concede that none of us is perfect. But that we all need a revolutionary change (such as the new birth implies) is a doctrine resisted without ceasing.

Yet the New Testament, which was the product of the Christian faith and which is our source of knowledge about it, uncompromisingly teaches that it was the hopeless condition of man that made the gospel necessary. Christ's words to Nicodemus about the necessity to be born anew in order to see the kingdom of God were evidently meant for all men. Nicodemus was a respected man, not a down-and-outer who had failed to make the grade in the moral standards of a religious society. So was Saul of Tarsus. Yet he confessed without false modesty "that Christ Jesus came into the world to save sinners. And I am the foremost of sinners" (1 Timothy 1:15). Peter, the Galilean fisherman, likewise had no illusions about his need when he stood in the presence of Christ and saw his power and glory: "Depart from me," he said, "for I am a sinful, man, O Lord" (Luke 5:8). Nor are these men exceptions to the rule. Throughout Christian history it is clear that those who had drunk most deeply of the Spirit of Christ were the ones who recognized their unworthiness and the infinite gap which divided their own nature (by natural birth) from the new nature (by spiritual birth).

The analogy between physical birth and the birth "from above" needs careful handling if we are to avoid confusion and error in the matter of needing to be born anew. I heard someone remark in a public meeting recently that it is a great mistake to think that children who have been brought up in a religious home and in the Christian church need to be born anew in order to be received into the fellowship of the church. "I wouldn't dream of receiving my own children into full membership of the family when they had always lived there," he argues. The illustration is evidently misplaced. For one thing, no one has ever been *called* to be born physically. The newborn baby is, in a sense, an object which is being manipulated, even if by hands of love. But the gospel *calls* men to faith. Its message is directed to the understanding, conscience, and will. Then again, physical birth is in accordance with the creator's natural laws, but spiritually a child from its earliest years isn't only born into a corrupted environment, but also reveals an inward rebellion against God's laws. So the question of reconciliation is real. Further, to accept passively the customs, religious and otherwise, of the family in which one has been brought up, is one thing. To adopt them as one's own in a personal and vital manner when one has reached the age of discernment and discretion is another. And it is evident that one may be living under the same roof as the rest of the family without "belonging" to it.

THE TEST OF GENUINE FAITH

The need for new birth is frequently confused with the question about the manner in which it takes place. Must the revolutionary change be traceable to a definite date? Does it require a sudden, violent turn in the experience of the new believer? Such questions are common in certain circles and they frequently occasion genuine concern. Clearly, many people are tempted to universalize their own particular experience and to assess the authenticity of every other by incidental factors which belong to theirs. To appeal to the pattern found in the New Testament can be misleading, because there we find the Faith proclaimed for the first time and therefore it could be heard only by those who had reached the years of understanding. But in succeeding generations children were born into the families of believers, and so what seemed a strange teaching to the first generation became the accepted truth to others. Yet this doesn't imply that the call of the gospel is less radical today in its character. What it means is that the first awakening to its call may not be retained in the memory in later years. It is neither the manner nor the memory of the birth of faith that constitutes its essence, but the fruit of it. In fact, Christ himself warns against the deception of the sudden. The seed that springs up without first going down is destined to death, like all superficial emotions (Matthew 13:5, 6).

So the genuine mark of the new birth isn't the memory of its date (any more than that can be the mark of physical birth), but one's present attitude to the gospel (with all it implies about God's holiness and purpose of man, and man's misery and perdition outside of divine mercy). It isn't necessary for anyone to recall days when he lived in the gutter in order to appreciate the contrast between such a life and one born from above — enough of the glitter remains in every one of us to provide a test of the heart's real priorities. The "old man," to use St. Paul's terminology, though crucified to the believer (Romans 6:6), certainly takes a long time to die within him (Ephesians 4:22). Hence, the earlier a person comes to faith, the greater should be his hatred later of all that opposes God's truth as made known in the gospel. Authentic faith grows, and the more one grows in true goodness, the more sensitive one is to the presence of evil in the heart. So the man on an express train who emerges from a tunnel suddenly, and the man who moves through it ever so slowly, come out into the same light and leave behind the same darkness. The vital factor is the direction, not the speed, of the movement. Faith also, in whatever manner it is born, recognizes that "God is light and in him is no darkness at all," and "If we say we have fellowship with him while we walk in darkness, we lie and do not live according to the truth" (1 John 1:5, 6). For the test of true faith isn't simply what a man holds in his head, but what he loves in his heart. And the test of what he loves in his heart is not what brings tears to his eyes, but what moves his will to action. What moved the will of God to action in the gospel was his love for the world. "By this we know love, that he *laid down his life* for us" (1 John 3:16).

HOW IS FAITH BORN?

Whether the believer can or cannot recall the moment when faith was born in him, the way that birth is made possible is clearly revealed in the gospel. To bring together the various factors (already noted, in some form or another, in preceding chapters) that constitute the new birth, we may consider them in the following order:

In the first place, faith is awakened by something which the believer has *heard*. It is God, therefore, who makes the first move. Man's own reflections, whether logical or mystical, can never lead him to knowledge either of his deepest need or of the secret of its satisfaction. It is in the gospel that man hears he is alienated from God through sin, that "the wages of sin is death" (Romans 6:23). In the gospel he hears how, through death, God has in Christ reconciled the world to himself (2 Corinthians 5:19). Neither a keen appreciation of the beauty of nature around us nor a deep sensitivity to the sacred character of the moral law within us, whatever blissful and solemn feelings they may produce in the soul, can bring us to a living fellowship with our Maker. This can only be effected by redemption, and redemption can only be known as it is heard in the gospel. Shadows of it are indeed seen in those ages that preceded the incarnation of the Christ, but redemption itself in all its glory was unveiled when in the fullness of time God sent forth his Son.

In the second place, faith is awakened by *the call to re-*

pentance. Christ opened his ministry with this call and commissioned his disciples to proclaim it to the whole world after his resurrection. No demand is more radical than the call to repent, for to repent isn't simply to admit that I've done wrong in this or that matter, but that *I myself* am in the wrong relationship with God. It's not, therefore, a matter of owning that I've slipped up now and then, but that I need to change the direction in which I'm traveling. Repentance is the opposite of self-justification, since it implies accepting God's view of myself. That's why the truly repentant heart sees sin as "exceeding sinful," not as a mistake or an inevitable phase in the growth process. Sin is the pride which says, "We do not want this man to reign over us" (Luke 19:14). Sin is the selfishness and dishonesty that claims for itself what rightfully belongs to another, thus requiting love with ingratitude.

Some play down the importance of repenting. They regard it at best as something that can be taken in stride, without the urgency of him who came "to call sinners to repentance." One reason for this half-hearted attitude to repentance is the adoption of a false standard of judgment. We compare ourselves with others around us, who belong to a corrupt world, and this has the effect of lulling us into a fictitious security. But the genuine searcher for truth will permit himself to be searched by the truth and won't be deceived by relative standards. Hence the apostle's solemn reminder that "we must all appear before the judgment seat of Christ" (2 Corinthians 5:10).

Another reason for ignoring the seriousness of the call to repentance is a mistaken idea of God's love. It is the glory of that love, we are told, that it accepts us unconditionally. And this, it would appear, even rules out the necessity of repentance as a requirement for forgiveness. Such reasoning reveals a confused conception both of repentance and of grace. It seems to regard repentance as something man *does,* rather than as an attitude of accepting. Repentance is a gift that God offers to man, not something man can produce of himself and to order. So to dispense with repentance is also to dispose of salvation itself. If the essence of salvation is restoration to fellowship with God, rather than only exemption from punishment, the unrepentant heart chooses to shut itself out of that fellowship.

"What partnership have righteousness and iniquity? Or what fellowship has light with darkness?" (2 Corinthians 6:14). Nor does the need for repentance set a limit to the reach of God's grace. Repentance is not a qualification for reconciliation, but the only means by which man can appropriate the grace which reconciles. Otherwise reconciliation, emptied of its moral content, would be devalued in the eyes of both heaven and earth.

IS ASSURANCE ARROGANT?

Last, faith comes to birth with *trusting.* This too is something revolutionary, since the trust in question isn't trust in oneself, but in divine grace mediated through Christ. This trust alone can inspire genuine assurance of salvation. Such assurance is often regarded as a mark of arrogance, of an inflated idea of one's own goodness. And this has evoked a reaction on the part of others, who claim that they prefer to suspend all speculation about their salvation until the results are known on the great day ahead. And isn't such modesty and humility more becoming to sinners such as ourselves? In fact, however, such "humility" would seem to be a subtle form of pride, for it assumes that in that day one *may* find that one has been good enough in God's sight to pass the celestial entrance examination.

But the believer who has heard the gospel of grace and believed it, doesn't need to wait for that day to know the result. He knows it *now.* He knows that of himself he has already failed. His only hope, therefore, lies not in himself but in what God has promised and performed for him in Christ. It is *he* who has given the assurance: "I give them eternal life, and they shall never perish, and no one shall snatch them out of my hand" (John 10:28). Now, if his words cannot provide grounds for our assurance, how can our works?

Nor is grace something that will be our confidence in that future time only. It is meant as the source of strength for the believer here and now, that he might "fight the good fight of faith" without succumbing to unbelief which dims his vision and robs him of energy. Grace enables him to "go boldly to the throne of grace" itself. Grace is able to keep him from falling. True, it's easier to talk about grace than to act on it. But that it's not mere talk is clear from the fact that it was precisely from those who had acted on it that we first learned about it.

Let it not be imagined that to trust in the grace of God, rather than in our own merits, is just an easy substitute for moral earnestness. Such trust entails a new attitude in facing facts, not less efforts in tackling them. Someone once told me that his life had gone to pieces and that his attempts at gaining forgiveness and peace of mind by doing good deeds had been of no avail. Even prayer left the heavens like lead: "I cannot get through," he remarked. But it was evident that the way of faith, the faith which trusts, was quite strange to him. It hadn't dawned on him that our faith is a gospel just because it is news of him who has got through to us when we've failed to get through to him. It's obvious that to the slave of fatal habit, like the man mentioned, the requirement of goodness as a condition of forgiveness would only cripple the tortured soul still more. St. Paul told us that the demands of the law plunged him into still deeper despair. It was when he heard "the word of the Cross," through which the grace of God flowed into a guilty world, that he saw the door open to a new life of freedom and power. For the curse of guilt is taken away *before* the cure of the affliction is effected. The peace that comes by trusting isn't the consequence of successful effort, but the precondition of it. We are "justified *freely* by his grace through the redemption that is in Christ" (Romans 3:24, KJV). Those words were written by the apostle who also said that "faith comes by hearing" (Romans 10:17, KJV). It's evident from the witness of his own life to the power of the gospel that this didn't mean that it comes by hearsay, which is only secondhand knowledge.

THE SOVEREIGNTY OF GRACE

In saying that faith is born through the stages of hearing, repenting and trusting, I don't mean that we can bring it to birth by observing a set of instructions, as a cook follows a recipe or a pharmacist makes up a prescription. For just as "the wind blows where it wills, and you hear the sound of it, but you do not know whence it comes or whither it goes; so it is with everyone who is born of the Spirit" (John 3:8).

Faith is the gift of sovereign grace. We know the infinite reach and power of that grace because of God's gift of Christ to the world. The fact of Christ enables faith to face all other facts, whether "things present" or "things to come" (Romans 8:38). And Christ declared, "Him who comes to me I will not cast out" (John 6:37).

Recommended Reading

For further study of many topics connected with the theme of this book, the following books are suggested. The asterisk denotes publications which do not assume much background of a technical nature in the field of philosophical theology. Other books are included in the separate notes on the text itself.

* Colin Brown: *Philosophy and the Christian Faith* (Inter-Varsity Press, 1969).

* Frederick Ferré: *Basic Modern Philosophy of Religion* (Scribner, 1967).

* Michael Green: *Runaway World* (Inter-Varsity Press, 1968).

* John Hick: *Philosophy of Religion* (Prentice-Hall, Inc., 1963).

J. H. Hick: *Arguments for the Existence of God* (Macmillan, 1970).

* H. D. Lewis: *Philosophy of Religion* (English Universities Press Teach Yourself, 1965).

* Geddes MacGregor: *Introduction to Religious Philosophy* (Macmillan, 1960).

* Thomas McPherson: *The Philosophy of Religion* (Van Nostrand, 1965).

* E. D. L. Miller: *God and Reason* (The Macmillan Company, New York, 1972).

H. P. Owen: *The Christian Knowledge of God* (Oxford U. Press, 1969).

H. J. Paton: *The Modern Predicament* (Humanities, 1962).

Notes

CHAPTER 1

1. Raymond Pannikar: *Theoria to Theory* (Hodder & Stoughton, Jan. 1967), p. 129.
2. Martin Buber, quoted by R. Gregor Smith: *Secular Christianity* (Collins), pp. 44-45.
3. J. Rickaby: *Scholasticism* (A. Constable, 1908), p. 27.
4. For a distinguished lawyer's assessment of the evidence for the Resurrection, see J. N. D. Anderson: *Christianity: the Witness of History* (Inter-Varsity Press, 1970).

CHAPTER 2

1. A. J. Ayer: *Language, Truth and Logic* (Dover, 2nd ed.).
2. cf. Nels F. S. Ferré: *Searchlights on Contemporary Theology* (Harper & Row).
3. *An Empiricist's View of the Nature of Religious Belief* (Cambridge University Press, 1955).
4. Flew & Macintyre: *New Essays in Philosophical Theology* (Macmillan, 1964).
5. *Ibid.*, p. 96.
6. E. H. Madden & P. H. Hare: *Evil and the Concept of God* (Thomas, Springfield, Illinois, 1968).
7. See Thomas McPherson: "Religion as the Inexpressible" (*New Essays in Philosophical Theology*), Ch. vii.
8. *What I Believe* (Allen & Unwin, 1966), pp. 235-236.
9. Austin Farrer: *Faith and Speculation* (N. Y. U. Press, 1967).
10. Quoted by Hugh Meynell in *Theology* (SPCK), Aug. 1965, p. 366.

CHAPTER 3

1. H. Bettenson: *Documents of Church History* (Oxford University Press), p. 8.
2. H. T. Kerr (ed.): *A Compendium of Luther's Theology* (Westminster Press, Philadelphia), p. 4.
3. *A Return to Natural Theology* (James Clarke, 1967), p. 219.
4. Dennis O'Brien in *Faith and the Philosophers* (Macmillan, 1964), ed. John Hick, p. 234.
5. *The Modern Predicament* (Humanities, 1955).
6. H. T. Kerr, *op. cit.*, p. 132.
7. *Ibid.*, p. cciv (italics mine).
8. A. J. Ayer, *op. cit.*, p. 118.
9. For an illuminating treatment of "God and Mystery," see H. D. Lewis in *Prospect for Metaphysics* (Allen & Unwin), ed. I. T. Ramsey; Ch. xii.
10. Cyril C. Richardson: *The Library of Christian Classics* (Macmillan, 1970), Vol. 1.
11. W. MacNeile Dixon: *The Human Situation* (Arnold, 1937), p. 21.
12. F. Waismann in *Contemporary British Philosophy* (Allen & Unwin, 3rd Series, 1956, ed. H. D. Lewis), p. 460.
13. Blaise Pascal: *Thoughts on Religion* — translation of "Les Pensées: Pascal" (Washington Square Press).

CHAPTER 4

1. Austin Farrer: *op. cit.*, p. 19.
2. P. W. Kent in *The Modern Churchman*, Oct. 1963.
3. "Science and the Catholic Tradition" (*Science and Religion*, Ian G. Barbour ed., (Harper & Row, 1968).
4. A. J. Ayer: *op. cit.*, p. 117.
5. *Science and Religion*, p. 300.
6. Quoted by G. H. Clark in *A Christian View of Men and Things* (Eerdmans, 1952), p. 199.
7. *Mysticism and Logic* (Barnes & Noble).
8. Collins, p. 74.
9. *The Spiritual Crisis of the Scientific Age* (Fernhill).
10. *Encyclopedia of Philosophy*, ed. Paul Edwards (New York, Macmillan), Vol. 5, p. 349.
11. G. D. Yarnold: *op. cit.*, p. 36.
12. See also H. D. Lewis: *Presidential Address to the Aristotelian Society*, 1962.

13. *Christianty in a Mechanistic Universe* (IVF Pocketbook, ed. D. M. Mackay), p. 29.
14. *Face to Face*: Hugh Burnett (ed.) (Jonathan Cape, 1964), p. 11.
15. Sir Bernard Lovell: *The Individual and the Universe* (OUP, 1961).
16. "Genetic Control and the Future of Man" (*Science and Religion, op. cit.*), p. 315.

CHAPTER 5

1. B. L. Manning: *Essays in Orthodox Dissent* (Independent Press), p. 28.
2. *Ibid.,* p. 29.
3. H. H. Farmer: *Revelation and Religion* (Nisbet, 1954), p. 195.
4. Oscar Cullmann: *Salvation in History* (SCM, 1965).
5. *Towards a Theology of History* (Mowbrays, 1965).
6. *Freedom and History* (Humanities).
7. John Macquarrie: *God-Talk* (Harper & Row, 1967).
8. *The Rationality of Faith* (Scribner).
9. C. A. Coulson: *Science and Christian Belief* (Oxford University Press, 1955), p. 40.
10. *The History of Europe* (Verry).
11. H. D. Lewis & R. L. Slater: *World Religions* (C. A. Watts, 1966), p. 173.
12. B. L. Manning: *op. cit.,* p. 41.

CHAPTER 6

1. For penetrating studies on issues connected with religious experience, see H. D. Lewis: *Our Experience of God* (Allen & Unwin); H. P. Owen: *The Christian Knowledge of God* (Oxford University Press, 1969); H. H. Price in *Faith and the Philosophers* (St. Martin Press, 1964, ed. John Hick); C. A. Campbell: *Godhood and Selfhood* (Humanities, 1957).
2. *Op. cit.,* p. 32.
3. *Arguments for the Existence of God* (Macmillan, 1970), p. 115.
4. A. J. Ayer: *op. cit.,* p. 106
5. Faith and the Philosophers (see note 1).
6. Terence Penelhum: *Problems of Religious Knowledge* (Macmillan, 1971), p. 140.
7. *Western Mail,* 9 April, 1968.
8. I have dealt more fully with this in a review on Madden & Hare: *op. cit.,* in *Religious Studies,* March 1971 (Cambridge University Press), ed. H. D. Lewis.

CHAPTER 7

1. *The Nature of Metaphysical Thinking* (Macmillan), p. 117.
2. Quoted by John Stott: *Christ the Controversialist* (Inter-Varsity Press, 1970).

CHAPTER 8

1. *The Elusive Mind* (Humanities, 1970).
2. Quoted by Carl Michalson: *op. cit.,* p. 125.
3. *Religion and Humanism* (BBC Publishers), pp. 64-65.
4. Cited by A. J. Ayer in *The Western Mail,* 9 April 1968.
5. *The Unity of Philosophical Experience* (Scribner).
6. *What is Faith?* (Eerdmans).